MARTIN OSTWALD

OLIGARCHIA

HISTORIA

ZEITSCHRIFT FÜR ALTE GESCHICHTE · REVUE D'HISTOIRE
ANCIENNE · JOURNAL OF ANCIENT HISTORY · RIVISTA
DI STORIA ANTICA

EINZELSCHRIFTEN

HERAUSGEGEBEN VON
MORTIMER CHAMBERS/LOS ANGELES · HEINZ HEINEN/TRIER
FRANÇOIS PASCHOUD/GENEVE · HILDEGARD TEMPORINI/TÜBINGEN
GEROLD WALSER/BASEL

HEFT 144

FRANZ STEINER VERLAG STUTTGART
2000

MARTIN OSTWALD

OLIGARCHIA

THE DEVELOPMENT
OF A CONSTITUTIONAL FORM
IN ANCIENT GREECE

FRANZ STEINER VERLAG STUTTGART
2000

Ostwald, Martin:
Oligarchia : the development of a constitutional form in ancient
Greece / Martin Ostwald. – Stuttgart : Steiner, 2000
   (Historia : Einzelschriften ; Bd. 144)
   ISBN 3-515-07680-8

ISO 9706

Jede Verwertung des Werkes außerhalb der Grenzen des Urheberrechtsgesetzes ist
unzulässig und strafbar. Dies gilt insbesondere für Übersetzung, Nachdruck, Mikroverfilmung oder vergleichbare Verfahren sowie für die Speicherung in Datenverarbeitungsanlagen. © 2000 by Franz Steiner Verlag Wiesbaden GmbH, Sitz Stuttgart. Gedruckt auf
säurefreiem, alterungsbeständigem Papier. Druck: Druckerei Proff, Eurasburg.
Printed in Germany

CONTENTS

Preface and Acknowledgments 7

Introduction 9

1. Constitutions: Early Classifications 13
2. The Rule of a Few and Ideology 21
3. Philosophical Revaluation: Plato 31
4. Theory and Practice: Aristotle 31
5. The Oligarchical Citizen in Aristotle 41
   a. The place of oligarchy 41
   b. Property and citizenship 44
   c. Property valuation 50
   d. "Well-to-do" and "indigent" in oligarchy and democracy 52
   e. Oligarchical wealth and public service 69
   f. The four kinds of oligarchy 70
   g. Conclusion: Oligarchical citizenship 71

Bibliography of Works Cited 77

Indices 81
   1. General Index 81
   2. Index Locorum 86
   3. Greek Index 95

PREFACE AND ACKNOWLEDGMENTS

What is now being published as a separate monograph was orginally designed as an introduction to an extended study of oligarchical states in ancient Greece of the classical period. When that study proved to be more intractable and time-consuming than I had anticipated, I decided that this introductory search for a definition of oligarchy might be suitable for publication in its own right. Although its most original contribution refines the terms in which Aristotle envisaged the citizen of an oligarchy, it also attempts to examine how his discussion is prefigured (a) by a growing Greek awareness of differences in the forms of human governance, which have helped shape modern conceptions of what is "political", and (b) by the views of oligarchy articulated by Aristotle's predecessors in the fourth and fifth centuries B.C.E.

In short, my aim is not to replace the work of L. Whibley (*Greek Oligarchies: Their Classification and Organisation* [London, 1896]), which despite its age has never yet been replaced, but to complement its typological orientation with a study of the problems the Greeks of the classical period encountered in their attempts to define oligarchy.

I am grateful to the Editors of *Historia* for having accepted this paper for publication and to Dr. Alexander F. Wensler for seeing it through the press. My thanks go especially to Professor Mortimer Chambers and to his predecessor, Professor Kurt A. Raaflaub, whose critical suggestions have made the work better than it was. I am grateful also to Professors Josiah Ober and William Turpin for their careful reading of the typescript and for the valuable criticisms they contributed. Fellowship support from the *National Endowment for the Humanities* enabled me to begin this study during a year's leave spent in 1990–91 under the stimulating auspices partly of the *Institute for Advanced Study* at Princeton, and partly of the *Centre Louis Gernet* of the *École des Hautes Études en Sciences Sociales* at Paris, where discussions with many colleagues, especially Professors Pierre Vidal-Naquet and Pauline Schmitt Pantel, were of inestimable value. To Professor Marcel Piérart I am indebted for having compelled me, by is invitation to lecture on oligarchy at the Université de Fribourg, to give some sort of coherence to my thoughts.

I am further indebted to Swarthmore College for a subvention to cover the cost of producing the 'Index Auctorum' and to Benjamin Lee for compiling it.

Swarthmore, PA, April 2000   Martin Ostwald

INTRODUCTION

The study of human history is the study of human societies and of the ways human beings organize themselves to live in a community. No human society has yet been discovered that lacks some form of governance. The study of what forms governance may take comes chronologically and logically only long after a form of government has been established, practised, and ingrained in the life of a given society. Why men need governing is less a question for historians than for psychologists. Historians can proceed from the assumption that government will have been instituted and accepted by members of a given society in response to exigencies in which it found itself. Only after government had become an established fact of human existence, and only after contact with other societies had created awareness of the existence of differences between different forms of governance prevailing in different societies, will self-conscious examination have discovered the existence of alternative forms of government, and thus the peculiar form of one's own.

This kind of development is fairly securely attested for the Greeks, who will be our concern here. The earliest intelligible documents in Greek attest the existence only of individual rulers, monarchs, in whom authority over social groups was vested. *Lawagetai* and *wanaktes* lorded it over the palaces of Knossos, Mycenae, and Pylos.[1] Kingship persisted as the norm of government through the so-called "Dark Age,"[2] and in the Homeric poems the various Greek contingents fighting before Troy have one noble ruler each. The expedition as a whole is commanded by an individual, Agamemnon, king of Mycenae, by reason of his superior military strength and of his blood-relation to the injured party, Menelaus, king of Sparta. The dominance of Odysseus' family in Ithaca and of Alcinous in Phaeacia seems to be based on a similar principle. Assemblies of tribal kings as well as of commoners could be convoked to advise, but final decisions remained the King's alone. When mutiny threatens his position, it is beaten down with the words: "a system of many masters is not good; let one be master, one be king, to whom the son of subtle-minded Kronos has given staff and authority to guide them in council."[3] Neither among Greek or non-Greek

---

[1] See Chadwick (1973) 618.
[2] See Drews (1983).
[3] Homer, *Il.* II. 204–6: οὐκ ἀγαθὸν πολυκοιρανίη· εἷς κοίρανος ἔστω, / εἷς βασι-

peoples is the existence of a rival system to monarchy envisaged.[4] The one kingless society we encounter, that of the Cyclopes, is regarded as uncivilized, even though it is blessed with natural bounty: reliance on divine providence makes the Cyclopes overconfident and anarchical; watered by rain from Zeus, the soil yields to them without cultivation wheat, barley, and grapes; they have no gatherings to deliberate about public affairs, and there is no authority established over them; what authority they recognize in their mountainous cave-dwellings is exercised by each man over his own wife and children, and without concern for their neighbors. (*Od.* IX. 106–14). We are here told of a society which, its enviable economic situation notwithstanding, lacks civilization. Civilized societies are ruled by a king.

This inference is supported by other testimony from the seventh and sixth centuries B.C.E. Hesiod, too, speaks only of kings as rulers over mankind, but the context leaves it unclear how many "kings" any one given society has.[5] There is no mention of conflict among kings. Monarchy in some form is not merely the earliest but the only form of government referred to in Greek lyric poetry. But the contexts in which it is found have little to do with government. Two fragments of Archilochus mention "tyranny", neither as the perverse form of monarchy in which we find it some centuries later, nor even as a description of rulers and their authority: in both cases it is something admired by most people for the wealth and power it brings, but rejected by the speaker in favor of simpler values.[6]

Soon after Archilochus, however, "tyranny" seems to have assumed a political meaning. It is applied by Alcaeus to Pittacus, the ruler over his native Mytilene in the early sixth century,[7] whom Alcaeus disliked intense-

λεύς, ᾧ δῶκε Κρόνου πάις ἀγκυλομήτεω/ σκῆπτρόν τ' ἠδὲ θέμιστας, ἵνα σφίσι βουλεύῃσι. Line 206 has been athetized by a number of editors, because (a) it does not appear in some manuscripts, and (b) where it appears it usually has the unmetrical βασιλεύῃ ("to be king over them") as its last word. The context is the mutiny that has broken out in the wake of Agamemnon's suggestion to give up the siege of Troy and return home. The arguments used by Odysseus to restrain the commoners from running away contain an interesting justification of monarchy: "You don't know what you are doing! Sit still and listen to what others tell you who are better than you. You are unwarlike and have no strength; you don't count at all when it comes to war and deliberation. Not all of us Achaeans here are going to be kings" (ib. 199–203).

[4] See Finley (1979) 79–82. For a full discussion, see Vlachos (1974), Chs. II-III.

[5] Hesiod, *Op.* 248–73. Cf. also the Homeric *Hymn to Demeter* 473–82, where Demeter teaches her rites to five kings of Eleusis.

[6] Archilochus, frr. 19 and 23.20 (West)

[7] Alcaeus, fr. 348 (L.-P.), cf also fr. 75 and μοναρχίαν fr. 6.27. See Page (1955) 149–52, and Cook (1982) 201.

ly. We know that the circumstances which gave rise to Pittacus' rule were quite different from those upon which Homeric kingship had been based. Late sources indicate that aristocratic family dynasties succeeded Homeric kings in most parts of the Greek world, and that it was from these that tyrannies developed.[8] We learn from Solon and Theognis that these were feared and disliked by the upper classes of Athens as well as of Megara in the first half of the sixth century.[9] The fact that no names for the rule by family dynasties have come down to us suggests that it was accepted as a phenomenon, and that apparently little thought was devoted to exploring its peculiarities and to comparing it with kingship and tyranny.

And finally, the fact that something which later came to be called "democracy" evolved from the reforms of Cleisthenes escaped his contemporaries. They celebrated the overthrow of the tyranny of the Peisistratids as having brought "political equality" to Athens, but if they gave any thought to the substance of that equality, we have little indication of it.[10]

It is no accident that we first encounter an awareness of the existence of different forms of government and an attempt to explore the differences among them in Herodotus, the inveterate fifth-century traveller and ethnographer, whose experiences made him draw the conclusion that, "if one were to present all social norms to all men and bid them to pick out the best from among them, upon examination each group would choose their own; so deeply ingrained is the conviction in each that their own norms are by far the best."[11] And, as we shall see, Herodotus is also the earliest extant author to use the terms "oligarchy" and "democracy." Although that does not mean that these terms had not gained currency earlier, it shows that by the time of Herodotus, that is, by the middle of the fifth century, they had become part of Greek political thinking. It is from Greek political thinking, as first articulated by Herodotus that Western political thought evolved.

To determine the place of oligarchy among the forms of government recognized by the Greeks is the purpose of this study. The only monograph that has been devoted to its study in the recent past is that by Leonard

---

[8] See Murray (1980) ch. 9.

[9] Solon, frr. 32.2, 33.6, 34.7 (West), cf. μονάρχου δουλοσύνην at 9.3–4; Theognis 823, 1181, and 1204.

[10] See the Attic skolia in Page (1962) 893.4 and 896.4 with Ostwald (1969) 96–136, and 137–60. The earliest appreciation of its value is Herodotus' praise of ἰσογορίη at V.78.

[11] Hdt. III.38.1: εἰ γάρ τις προθείη πᾶσι ἀνθρώποισι ἐκλέξασθαι κελεύων νόμους τοὺς καλλίστους ἐκ τῶν πάντων νόμων, διασκεψάμενοι ἂν ἑλοίατο ἕκαστοι τοὺς ἑωυτῶν· οὕτω νομίζουσι πολλόν τι καλλίστους τοὺς ἑωυτῶν νόμους ἕκαστοι εἶναι.

Whibley, published in 1896.[12] As a typological study of oligarchy and the forms it took in ancient Greece, it remains irreplaceable and a mine of information. Newer archaeological and epigraphical discoveries, their interpretations, and more recent methods of looking at Greek social organizations make it desirable to bring Whibley's work up to date. That task would depend on a major effort than I am prepared to undertake here. My aim is, rather, to complement Whibley's typological analysis with a historical account of how oligarchy was perceived and evaluated by the Greeks from its first emergence to the time of Aristotle.

We shall attempt to understand oligarchy not as a fixed type of government, but as product of varying and shifting views, especially of property, current in classical Greece. This understanding depends largely on a new look at Aristotle, who tells us more about oligarchy, both as a social theory and as a historical and economic reality than any other Greek author. We shall examine what steps led up to the differentiations between the various forms of government in ancient Greece, and how in reaction to them Aristotle gave us the most coherent picture we have of what "oligarchy" meant to the Greeks.

---

[12] Whibley (1896).

1. CONSTITUTIONS: EARLY CLASSIFICATIONS

The classification of different possible régimes into the rule of one, the rule of a few, and the rule of the many, which we have inherited from the Greeks, has become such a commonplace in Western civilization that we tend to forget how uniquely Greek it is. It is true that, in retrospect, democratic and oligarchical features can be detected in the usually monarchical empires of the ancient Near East; but more often than not such features have been identified only where the original sources have come to us filtered through Greek minds, as they have, for example, in Herodotus' account of the origin of the kingship of Media. Deioces is said to have become king over the Medes through appointment by an assembly of the Medes, in which debate took place, having first been "elected" (αἱρέοντο) as judge in his village;[13] however, there is nothing in the native traditions of Media, Persia, or any other Near Eastern country which envisages a government in which decisions in public matters are arrived at by a popular assembly through debate as an alternative to the kind of monarchical rule to which each state was respectively accustomed.

The uniqueness of the Greek classification can be seen even more strikingly in cases in which we depend entirely on Near Eastern sources for our information. For example, the appointment of Saul as king over the Israelites is preceded at Samuel II 8:4–5 by the despatch of a delegation from a gathering of Elders to Samuel requesting him to "appoint for us a king to govern us like all the nations," a request interpreted by the voice of the Lord at verse 7 as emanating from "the voice of the people." Although the aim of the petition, the establishment of a monarchy, is clear enough, there is little else in this account that can be understood from a Greek perspective. There is, in the first place, no Greek analogue to the position of Samuel as an individual endowed with absolute authority to make the appointment; the closest Greek parallel is the appointment by Apollo's Oracle at Delphi of an *oikistes* to lead a colony overseas, of a lawgiver to

---

[13] Hdt. I. 96. 2, and esp. 97. 2–3: συνελέχθησαν οἱ Μῆδοι ἐς τὠυτὸ καὶ ἐδίδοσαν σφίσι λόγον... φέρε στήσωμεν ἡμέων αὐτῶν βασιλέα.... Polyaenus VII. 1 has the people "vote" only to give him a bodyguard, with whose help he then proceeded to make himself king; cf. the accounts of Peisistratus' accession to tyranny at Hdt. I. 59. 5–6 and Arist., *Ath.Pol.* 14. 1.

give a code of laws to his city, or perhaps of the elusive ἐξηγηταὶ πυθόχρηστοι,[14] but these are usually men already nominated for the purpose by the petitioning community. Secondly, the deliberating Elders in *Samuel* II seem to be an oligarchical body which, strangely enough, cannot authenticate – to say nothing of implement – the decision it has taken; it can merely petition the man of God, presumably – and on this point we can only guess in the absence of any information – without appeal or other recourse, if their petition should be denied. And thirdly, there is even a question whether the Elders can be regarded as an oligarchical body, since God Himself defines their petition as the (democratic) voice of the people. "The central concerns of political philosophy as the Greeks understood it – the best régime, ruling and being ruled, the meaning of citizenship, the deliberative process, civic virtue, political obligation – were never central in Israelite thought. We can, maybe, tease out perspectives and positions relevant to these concerns, but we can't find arguments."[15]

What is true of Persia and Israel is also true of Egypt, of the Mesopotamian city-states, of the Assyrians, Hittites, Phoenicians, and other societies of the ancient Near East.[16] It is also true of the Romans until they took the classification of the forms of government over from the Greeks, presumably first through Polybius (VI. 3–4).

In view of this, it is strange that the first explicit appearance of a tripartite classification is found in what purports to be a Persian context, the so-called "Constitutional Debate", which Herodotus (III. 80–82) assigns to three of the seven conspirators, after they had successfully overthrown the rule of the false Smerdis.[17] The Greek cast of the setting and the Greek character of the ideas and arguments presented by the three Persian participants have caused several modern scholars to disregard Herodotus' twice-repeated avowal of the accuracy of his report (III. 80. 1 and VI. 43. 3) and to reject the very notion that a similar debate may indeed have taken place among the successful conspirators. I have argued elsewhere that such arguments are inadequate to deny the Constitutional Debate a claim to

---

[14] See Jacoby (1949) 28–38; Oliver (1950) 36–46.

[15] Walzer, *Biblical Politics*, Ch. XIII, p. 10; cf also Ch. XII, p. 1: "Politics is not recognized by any of the biblical writers as a centrally important or humanly fulfilling activity." I wish to use this opportunity to express my deep gratitude to Professor Walzer for letting me read this unpublished work.

[16] See, for example, the two articles by Jacobsen (1970a and 1970b) republished in Moran (1970) 157–70 and 132–56. In general, see Glassman (1986).

[17] For a recent discussion, which, however, strangely substitutes "aristocracy" for the "oligarchy" of the Debate, see Bleicken (1979) 148–72, esp. 151–8. ἀριστοκρατία does not occur in Herodotus.

historicity altogether.[18] Since the conspirators had created a constitutional vacuum, which needed to be filled, it is not unreasonable to believe that their deliberations on that problem produced discussions in 522/1 B.C.E., a watered-down report of which may well have reached Herodotus through Greek informants. Using their account as the historical nucleus of the debate, he may then have adumbrated it with arguments of his own construction. We shall turn to these arguments presently.

There is an indication that a tripartite classification is not Herodotus' invention, but that it had become part of Greek thinking at some earlier point. We encounter it first in Pindar some three or four decades before Herodotus.[19] What he says is too terse and enigmatic to be explained by its context:

ἐν πάντα δὲ νόμον εὐθύγλωσσος ἀνὴρ προφέρει,
παρὰ τυραννίδι, χὠπόταν ὁ λάβρος στρατός,
χὠταν πόλιν οἱ σοφοὶ τηρέωντι.

("A man straightforward in speech brings forward social order to everything he does, both under a tyranny, and when the boisterous host, and when the wise watch over the city").[20]

The remarkable feature of these lines is that they are completely apolitical: the emphasis is on an individual who, by freely speaking his mind, brings order into his society regardless of the kind of régime under which he lives. The focus is on the man: the three forms of government mentioned are incidental, perhaps irrelevant, to Pindar's concern.

Pindar merely observes the three forms of government without ranking or evaluating them; he simply states that none of the three inhibits the upright man from fostering order in his society. No opprobrium is attached to τυραννίδι, which refers unequivocally to one-man rule. Pindar's very

---

[18] See Ostwald (1969) 178–9; see also Asheri (1990) 295–7 with recent bibliography. For the Persian perspective on the Constitutional Debate, see Sancisi-Weerdenburg (1980) 230–38.

[19] The precise date of Pindar, *Pythians* II is still controversial and likely to remain so. Most scholars favor *ca.* 470 B.C.E. (see Burton [1962] 114–15; Maehler [1987] 55 reluctantly suggests 475 B.C.E. without argument; while Bowra [1964] 410 opts for 468 B.C.E.). Whatever date we adopt for the composition of Herodotus' work, *Pythians* II will be at least three or four decades earlier.

[20] Pind. *Pyth*. II. 86–88. For justification of this translation, see Ostwald (1969) 30–1 with n. 4. Bleicken's interpretation (1979) 150 n. 4, that "der aufrichtige Mann sich gemäß den gewünschten Verhaltensnormen verhält, einerlei welche Gruppen oder Personen in der Stadt gerade das Übergewicht haben," is made untenable by Pindar's use of προφέρει: it is the "man straightforward in speech" who sets the tone, not those in power.

rare mention of "tyrants" and "tyranny" elsewhere suggests that τυραννίδι is here to be taken as value-neutral: for Pindar, the distinguishing feature of a tyrant is his prosperity (*Pyth.* III. 85), but he is aware that this is a brittle foundation for a régime and may not last (*Pyth.* XI. 53);[21] there is no indication as to whether it is exercised in a brutal or a gentle fashion.

It is easier to feel confident that Pindar meant οἱ σοφοί to refer to a government by the few than to be sure whom he identifies as σοφοί. For Pindar, σοφός is usually a knowledgeable expert, and σοφία is the expertise with which he is endowed; frequently the terms describe, respectively, the poet and his craft. The latter sense is obviously not applicable in the present instance, and there is nothing to suggest that Pindar regarded "wisdom" as the prerogative of the wealthy or the nobly born, from among whom the few are usually recruited in later political thinking. Moreover, to think of Pindar's σοφοί as constituting an intellectual or cultural élite is anachronistic,[22] since in Greek archaic thought σοφία is invariably also expressed in action. In the absence of persuasive parallels in Pindar's writings, it is perhaps not too daring to think of the semi-legendary Seven Wise Men (Ἑπτὰ Σοφοί) as analogous, and to assume that Pindar regarded a government of such *maîtres de la vérité* as the rule of a few. There is nothing derogatory and perhaps even something laudatory about οἱ σοφοί.

Moreover, στρατός has no pejorative associations. But how are we to take the adjective λάβρος? Pindar uses it elsewhere of a force or a person difficult to bridle: of the dense smoke issuing forth from a city under siege (*Ol.* VIII. 36), of the flames of a pyre (*Pyth.* III. 40), of the jaws of the dragon that guarded the Golden Fleece (*Pyth.* IV. 244), and of the forwardness of people who pour forth verbiage without control, because they have no natural ability to write poetry (*Ol.* II. 87). If the addition of λάβρος makes the domination of the στρατός less desirable than that of the σοφοί in that it is uncouth rather than cultivated, Pindar does not explicitly say so. It may here well imply more ebullience than lack of discipline, and may suggest that Pindar was thinking of the rule of the many in terms of "le schéma idéal d'une république des hoplites"[23] rather than in terms of democracy as it had developed by the time Herodotus wrote.

Pindar's tone makes it unlikely that he was the inventor of a tripartite classification into governments of one, of a few, and of the many; more probably he inherited it from a time beyond his memory or that of his

---

[21] Cf. Archilochus, frr. 19 and 23.20 (West). See Burton (1962) 71–3.

[22] Burton (1962) 7 suggests that Pindar has a cultural aristocracy in mind and compares *Pyth.* IX. 78 and IV. 295, where he interprets the σοφοί as an audience of connoisseurs.

[23] I borrow this expression from Vidal-Naquet (1968) 166.

contemporaries. But it is significant that we encounter it only among the Greeks in antiquity. The content Pindar gave it was to remain unique, but we do not encounter the formal distinctions until Herodotus embodied them in the Constitutional Debate in the form in which they entered later political thought.

To describe the rule of one, Herodotus uses in the Constitutional Debate all the terms found in later tradition: μούναρχος, τύραννος, and βασιλεύς for the person, and μουναρχίη, τυραννίς, and βασιληίη for the institution. ὀλιγαρχίη is the sole expression for the rule of a few. The rule exercised by the many is called δημοκρατέεσθαι in a later reference to Otanes' speech (VI. 43. 3), but remarkably enough, the term does not occur in any of the speeches of the Constitutional Debate. Otanes himself introduces the rule of the many as πλῆθος ἄρχον (III. 80.6: "the masses ruling"), a term taken up by both his interlocutors, who also use δῆμος ("people"). Megabyzus defines its ruling element also as ὅμιλος ("crowd"), but he uses the same term, too, of the ruling element in the oligarchy he favors.

The new element in Herodotus is that he presents the three constitutional forms in a context that demands evaluation. Each participant speaks not as a theorist but as an activist intent on persuading his fellow conspirators that the constitutional form he favors is the best for Persia. In light of this, it is noteworthy for the valuation of the rule of one that the μουναρχ- stem is used exclusively by Darius, who advocates it, and by his main opponent, Otanes, champion of the rule of the many, who, however, once uses τύραννος. Only Megabyzus, the advocate of the rule of a few, confines himself exclusively to the τυραν-stem in opposing one-man rule. Since for Otanes the μουναρχ- stem describes the sole ruler only before he becomes corrupted, we may infer that μουναρχ- has positive or at least neutral connotations; this tallies with other uses of the stem in Herodotus. And since Herodotus, both in his own name and in the speech given to Megabyzus calls the ruler τύραννος only at the point when prosperity leads him to ὕβρις and makes him turn against his fellow citizens (III. 80. 4 and 81. 2), we are tempted to infer purely pejorative overtones for the τυραν- stem;[24] however, we have to make allowance for the fact that one quality Otanes attributes to a tyrant is identical with what Archilochus and Solon had already predicated of him:[25] an unbecoming jealousy, in view of the fact that he already has all

[24] The long-prevailing view, best expressed by Andrewes (1963) 20–30, esp. 27, that Herodotus has no sharp distinction between μούναρχος, βασιλεύς, and τύραννος, needs to be modified in the light of Ferrill (1978) 385–98, who, however, goes to extremes in attributing a pejorative sense to τύραννος.
[25] See Archilochus, fr. 19. 3 (West), and Solon, fr. 33. 6 (West).

good things.²⁶ In short, Otanes seems to regard a τύραννος basically as a person whose power enables him to get anything he wants; but, paradoxically enough, his high position tends to make him oppressive, and turns him from a μούναρχος into a τύραννος.

The terms "king" (βασιλεύς) and "kingship" (βασιληίη) are used to describe the rule of one man only after the reestablishment of monarchy has been decided upon (III. 83. 2 and 84. 1–3), and, therefore, seem to describe the institution of monarchy as adopted by a given state as an institutional fact rather than a characterization of the monarch.

The positive qualities of one-man rule are confined to the speech of Darius: the rule by one good man inspires confidence in the people and best ensures that his plans are kept secret from enemies;²⁷ he further asserts that the Persians owe their political independence and its continuity to the rule of one man.²⁸ A much stronger case against one-man-rule is made out by Otanes: a single ruler is prone to overbearing arrogance (ὕβρις), a point seconded by Megabyzus (III. 80. 2–3; 81. 1); he is not accountable for his conduct (80.3), so that he begrudges the best men their survival, ignores social conventions, violates women, and kills men without trial (80. 3–5).

Otanes makes no comment, positive or negative, on government by a few. Its advocate, Megabyzus, and its opponent, Darius, call it ὀλιγαρχίη (III. 81. 1; 82. 1, 3, 4).²⁹ Megabyzus favors it, because it will be dominated by an "élite assemblage of the best men,"³⁰ which will include the conspirators, and he believes that "the best" have the best policies. The weakness of this argument consists not only in its failure to define the sense of "best" and in its special pleading. As Darius points out, when in an oligarchy many vie to give their best to promote the public good, rivalries for leadership will lead to private enmities and murderous civil discord to end in the establishment of monarchy, which is the true rule of "the best" (82.3).

The strongest positive arguments in favor of the rule of the many are put into the mouth of Otanes. He praises it as an open society, in which the

²⁶ Hdt. III. 80. 4: καίτοι ἄνδρα γε τύραννον ἄφθονον ἔδει εἶναι, ἔχοντά γε πάντα τὰ ἀγαθά.

²⁷ Id. III.82.2: ἀνδρὸς γὰρ ἑνὸς τοῦ ἀρίστου οὐδὲν ἄμεινον ἂν φανείη· γνώμῃ γὰρ τοιαύτῃ χρεώμενος ἐπιτροπεύοι ἂν ἀμωμήτως τοῦ πλήθεος, σιγῷτό τε ἂν βουλεύματα ἐπὶ δυσμενέας ἄνδρας οὕτω μάλιστα.

²⁸ Id. III.82.5. ἐλευθερίη in this political context surely denotes the absence of foreign domination; I here translate as "continuity" πατρίους νόμους μὴ λύειν ἔχοντας εὖ. See Ostwald (1995) 35–63, esp. 42–51.

²⁹ I cannot agree with the historical presuppositions posited by Bleicken (1979) 169–71 for an origin of the term ὀλιγαρχία in the opposition to democracy by states on which the Athenians had arbitrarily imposed it. See also n. 17 above.

³⁰ Hdt. III.81. 3: ἀνδρῶν τῶν ἀρίστων ἐπιλέξαντες ὁμιλίην.

masses rule; as bearing "the fairest name of all, *isonomie* (political equality); as electing magistrates by lot and holding them answerable for their official acts; and as arriving openly at public decisions.[31] Its negative aspects are stated by Megabyzus alone: the masses are useless, unintelligent, and prone to an excess (ὕβρις) which springs from the people's lack of discipline.[32] Darius concurs with Megabyzus and adds that popular rule invariably encourages cabals of evil-minded men to act against the common good.[33]

It is noteworthy that the criterion by which Herodotus judges régimes in the Constitutional Debate – assuming that the composition of the Debate in the form in which we have it accurately reflects his thinking – is the degree to which they perpetrate or avoid ὕβρις (excess); whether this justifies the opinion that his criterion is religious remains doubtful.[34] None of the interlocutors accuse oligarchy of fostering ὕβρις; but this consideration does not tip any scales in favor of oligarchy. Oligarchy is the least well-defined and least colorful of the three constitutions. The rule of one and the rule of many are both tainted with ὕβρις. The excesses of the latter are defined by Megabyzus as consisting in lack of intelligence and lack of discipline; but the excesses of one-man rule are criticized most severely by Otanes as engendered by the tyrant's prosperity and as consisting in a jealousy that makes him reject conventions, violate women, and kill men without trial. The absence of any reference to ὕβρις by Darius may be interpreted as reflecting Herodotus' own belief that this vice is so endemic to a monarchy that it cannot be argued away, and that he envisaged the opposition of tyranny and democracy to be the historically most significant. It may, therefore, be part of Herodotus' strategy to interpret the Persian

---

[31] Ibid. 80. 6, where the salient expressions are: πλῆθος ἄρχον, οὔνομα πάντων κάλλιστον...ἰσονομίην, πάλῳ ἀρχὰς ἄρχει, ὑπεύθυνον ἀρχὴν ἔχει, βουλεύματα πάντα ἐς τὸ κοινὸν ἀναφέρει.

[32] Ibid. 81. 1: ὁμίλου γὰρ ἀχρηίου οὐδέν ἐστι ἀξυνετώτερον οὐδὲ ὑβριστότερον; 81. 2: ...ἐς δήμου ἀκολάστου ὕβριν πεσεῖν.

[33] Ibid. 82. 4: δήμου τε αὖ ἄρχοντος ἀδύνατα μὴ οὐ κακότητα ἐγγίνεσθαι· κακότητος τοίνυν ἐγγινομένης ἐς τὰ κοινὰ ἔχθεα μὲν οὐκ ἐγγίνεται τοῖσι κακοῖσι, φιλίαι δὲ ἰσχυραί· οἱ γὰρ κακοῦντες τὰ κοινὰ συγκύψαντες ποιεῦσι.

[34] See, e.g., Apffel (1957) 48–49 with 48 nn. 2 and 3; Gammie (1986) 174–7 with n. 22. However, the exhaustive and intelligent discussion of ὕβρις by Fisher (1992) esp. 142–48, demonstrates that "whether the *hybris* involved in acts of impiety is conceived as being directed against the gods, the relations between gods and men in a community, or against the laws and values of the community and the beliefs of its members, it is in all cases *hybris* because it focuses on the insult done to those powers and to the humans upholding preservation of proper relations between gods and men" (p. 148). For the application of this to Herodotus, see ibid. 343–85.

Wars as a moral issue in which the ὕβρις of the Persian monarchy faced the more open society of the Greeks. Oligarchy played little or no part in the conflict between East and West.

Despite several modifications in the nature and number of constitutions posited, Herodotus' tripartite scheme remained the basis of all further developments in constitutional theory down to the time of Polybius and beyond.[35] But attempts to find criteria other than the perpetration and avoidance of ὕβρις made the path this development followed anything but straight.

---

[35] For a good discussion, see de Romilly (1959). The tripartite classification is still found in Plutarch's fragmentary essay *De unius in re publica dominatione, populari statu et paucorum imperio*, (*Moralia* 826a–827c). The genuineness of the tract is doubted by Ziegler (1951) 823–4.

2. THE RULE OF A FEW AND IDEOLOGY

Herodotus had made his classification of constitutions subservient to underlining what he regarded as a central issue in the Persian Wars: the conflict between an open and free society prevailing among the Greeks and the closed tyrannical society of Persia, an issue of the Greeks' fight for freedom against slavery under the Persians. In doing so, he had made "the few," as Pindar had done (pp. 15–17 above), members of the upper classes whose title to rule is based on birth and/or achievement.[36] Included in this group are the "the best men," whose "aggregate" (ἀνδρῶν τῶν ἀρίστων ὁμιλίην) Megabyzus envisaged as constituting the oligarchy he advocated as a possible successor to the rule of the false Smerdis in Persia (pp. 18–20 above).

After Herodotus, constitutional forms continued to be used for purposes of political propaganda. Within Athens the only propaganda we hear of redounds to the praise of democracy. Between the time of Cleisthenes and the 420s, we hear of dissatisfaction with the democratic régime, but not of any serious attempt to replace it.[37] What opposition there is to democracy usually comes from the outside and is envisaged as tyranny, as it is, for example, in Euripides' *Supplices* (403–55),[38] not as governmernt by the few or oligarchy.

There are, however, indications that by the time the *Supplices* was produced in 423 B.C.E. oligarchy had already entered the lists as the ideological opposite of democracy in internal matters. The evidence is found in Thucydides' account of civil strife on the island of Corcyra, where oligarchy and democracy had become political factions. Thucydides avoids using these tags, but presents the democrats as promoting their goals by the

---

[36] Unfortunately, the terms expressing "excellence" (ἀρετή, ἄριστος) leave it unclear whether the reference is to noble birth or great achievement. It may well be that Herodotus plays on this ambivalence in having Megabyzus use it of the rulers in an oligarchy, and Darius of the monarch.

[37] Plut., *Arist.* 13. 1, reports a conspiracy of impoverished members of distinguished families to overthrow the Athenian democracy just before the battle of Plataea; and Thuc. I. 107. 4–6 mentions some Athenians who, in 458/7 tried to persuade the Spartans to overthrow the democracy. On these events, see Ostwald (1986) 176–8.

[38] It is very unlikely that this passage prefigures the conflation of oligarchy and tyranny, the fear of which, according to Thuc. VI. 60. 1, dominated Athens in the wake of the profanation of the Mysteries in 415 B.C.E.

slogan "constitutional government with the equal sharing of rights by the masses" (πλήθους τε ἰσονομίας πολιτικῆς), and the oligarchs as advocating "government by the best men, which is responsible by reason of preferment" (ἀριστοκρατίας σώφρονος προτιμήσει) (Thuc. III. 82. 8).[39] Propaganda tags are used in place of dispassionate descriptions.

The foundations of party politics are laid in the Funeral Oration, when Thucydides has Pericles define "democracy" not in terms of a ruling class, but with an eye to the governed whose interest public policy is intended to serve: "democracy," according to Pericles, derives its name from the fact that it is administered "not with a view to a few but with a view to a greater number;" in terms of a later "funeral oration" it is "government for the people" rather than "government by the people."[40] The obvious inference is that an oligarchy governs in the interest of a few. In other words, the criteria for defining governments are set neither by moral considerations (such as avoidance or perpetration of ὕβρις) nor by the economic status of those in power, but by the interest of those who are being governed. We have here an anticipation of Socrates' response to Thrasymachus' argument in Plato's *Republic* that good government is aimed at the good of the governed.[41]

It is from this perspective that the slogans of the parties embroiled in conflict in Corcyra are to be understood. Neither side does – nor can afford to – state its aims in an honest and straightforward manner. Each hides its self-interest behind exaggerated and specious claims of its goals to create a public image by which it hopes to win people over to its side. The oligarchs disguise their intentions by advocating an élitist government by the best (ἀριστοκρατία), while the democrats promise a constitutional government with political equality.[42] We need not be surprised to find a political opposition which Thucydides expresses in prose through the polarities "masses"-"best" or "democracy"-"oligarchy" appearing in contemporary tragedy as opposition between democracy and tyranny; on the one hand, prose demands a greater degree of realism than poetry; on the other, references to oligarchy would not sit well in the heroic context of myth.

Oligarchy and tyranny appear combined as opponents of democracy for the first time in surviving literature in Thucydides' description of the

[39] For this interpretation, see Graham and Forsythe (1984) 25–45.
[40] Thuc. II. 37. 1: καὶ ὄνομα μὲν διὰ τὸ μὴ ἐς ὀλίγους ἀλλ' ἐς πλείονας οἰκεῖν δημοκρατία κέκληται. On the interpretation, see Rusten (1989) 145. The objections of Harris (1992) 163–65, fail to carry conviction.
[41] Pl.. *Resp.* I. 341a–342e; see below, pp. 31, 38.
[42] It is peculiar that ἀριστοκρατία, which is not attested before Thucydides (III. 82. 8 and VIII. 64. 3), is both times used in an ironic sense; see Andrewes (1981) 158; cf. also Debrunner (1947). 14.

atmosphere spread in Athens as a result of the profanation of the Mysteries on the eve of the departure of the fleet to Sicily (Thuc. VI. 60. 1). The two are not differentiated from one another in terms of the threat they were thought to constitute against the Athenian democracy, presumably because the fears aroused remained vague. The political prominence of Alcibiades and his alleged participation in the profanations will have engendered fear of tyranny; the involvement of so many young members of the upper class in both the profanations and the desecration of the Herms will have bred the suspicions that a conspiracy was afoot to replace the democracy with an oligarchy. However, the context is not sufficiently focused to help us identify what substance contemporaries would have attributed to the terms involved.

By the middle of the fifth century, ὀλιγαρχία (oligarchy) had been adopted as the regular term to describe government of the few.[43] There is little attempt to identify "the few" explicitly. The earliest occurrences in Herodotus leave "oligarchy" indistinguishable from "aristocracy", although it is never referred to as ἀριστοκρατία: as already noted, in the Constitutional Debate (III. 81. 3) ὀλιγαρχία is equated with an "aggregate of the best men" (ἀνδρῶν τῶν ἀρίστων ὁμιλίην), leaving it undetermined whether the "best" are so by birth or by merit;[44] to this we can add its only other use in Herodotus (V. 92β. 1) to describe the rule of the Bacchiads over Corinth, where we may presume it to refer to a rule by the nobly born.

After Herodotus, ὀλιγαρχία tends to become the exclusive antonym of δημοκρατία, and statements about its characteristics and those of its rulers begin to appear. The author of the pseudo-Xenophontic *Constitution of the Athenians*, whose anti-democratic stance has earned him in modern times the sobriquet "Old Oligarch," praises oligarchy explicitly as a better treaty-partner than democracy because it has a small number of guarantors of the provisions of the contract, and as a better and more honest home for anyone who is not a man of the people.[45] The adjectives he uses to describe the "few" tell us that oligarchs are "solid" (χρηστοί), "rich" (πλούσιοι), "no-

---

[43] Raaflaub (1989) 37–41 intimates that an oligarchical vocabulary developed in opposition to the democratic policies of Pericles. The passages in Pindar (above, pp. 15–17) and in Herodotus (above, pp. 17–18) make this hard to believe. Hölkeskamp (1998) argues, suggestively but, in my opinion, not convincingly, that political conflict consisted in the fifth century in individual aristocrats trying to win the *demos* over their side, and that the polarity "oligarchy-democracy" does not antedate Aristotle's school.

[44] See above, p. 21 with n. 36. Raaflaub (1989) 42, interprets Megabyzus' position as tantamount to "aristocracy."

[45] [Xen.], *Ath.Pol.* II. 17 and 20. In fact, it is likely that the "oligarchical" element in Athens developed in deliberate opposition to the established democracy. For some astute observations, see Raaflaub (1998a) 21–22.

ble" (γενναῖοι), "very influential" (δυνατώτατοι), and "very sophisticated" (δεξιώτατοι). From the negative characteristics attributed to the Athenian democracy we may infer that their positive counterparts characterize oligarchy: from his complaint that in Athens the common people are better off than the noble and the rich, in that all are eligible for allotted and elective office and all can speak freely, we may infer that an oligarchy would favor the noble and the rich, restrict eligibility to office, and inhibit free speech (I. 2). From various other statements we may conclude that an oligarchy bars the lower classes from membership in councils and assemblies and from addressing the public at political gatherings (I. 6, 9), and that it does a better job of controlling the conduct of slaves and metics (I. 10–12). However, it does not follow that he wants to generalize his complaints about democratic indiscipline, injustice, and unscrupulousness (I. 5) into the prevalence of excellence, wisdom, and education (I. 6–9) in oligarchies. The most glaring distinction between the two régimes, in the eyes of the Old Oligarch, seems to be between government in the interest of the poor and government in the interest of the rich. Wealth becomes here, presumably for the first time, an explicit hallmark of the few, but not the only one.

In Thucydides the opposition of oligarchy and democracy in characterizing a given régime is more overt and more pronounced. We get the earliest and most striking intimation of its importance in Diodotus' statement that in all allied cities "the δῆμος is well-disposed towards Athens, and either does not join the ὀλίγοι in revolt, or, if compelled to do so, is automatically an enemy to the defectors."[46] Oligarchical or democratic ideology is seen as a more potent bond than patriotism, and reaches across the boundaries of the state. Social and economic factors dominate not only internal but also external policy to a greater extent than political bonds.

If we can assign a precise chronology to ideological developments, Thucydides saw in the revolt on Corcyra a turning point which turned democracy and oligarchy into polar opposites, to indicate that the war was assuming an ideological dimension, which was to reach its climax in the internal turmoil in Athens in 411 B.C.E. He makes it abundantly clear that oligarchies developed an affinity to Sparta and democracies to Athens, that henceforth served as a basis for relating conflicts within states to the Peloponnesian War as a whole. It is no coincidence that the ὀλιγαρχ-stem, which occurs 9 times in Books I–VI, is found 32 times in Book VIII; while δημοκρατ-, found 14 times in Books I–VII, has 18 occurrences in Book VIII. Thucydides even goes so far as to have Nicias intimate that one of

---

[46] Thuc. III. 47. 2: νῦν μὲν γὰρ ὑμῖν ὁ δῆμος ἐν πάσαις ταῖς πόλεσιν εὔνους ἐστί, καὶ ἢ οὐ ξυναφίσταται τοῖς ὀλίγοις ἤ, ἐὰν βιασθῇ, ὑπάρχει τοῖς ἀποστήσασι πολέμιος εὐθύς .

Sparta's war-aims was to weaken her enemy by installing an oligarchical government at Athens.[47] But he takes it for granted that his audience knows what he is talking about: we learn little about the nature of oligarchy from his account of the suspicions of an oligarchical conspiracy aroused by the profanations of 415 B.C.E. (VI. 60. 1) and of the oligarchical activities of 411 B.C.E., except that it is a political movement, sponsored largely by members of the upper class (VIII. 47. 2), which employs conspiratorial and violent means in its attempts to overthrow the democracy; the specific proposals advanced at the infamous Colonus meeting yield no more than the presumption that payment for office was not on oligarchical agenda.[48] There is, however, something of substance in Athenagoras' speech at Syracuse (VI. 39). Though delivered in a partisan spirit, it mentions qualities objectively believed to differentiate oligarchy from democracy: oligarchy is predicated on the conviction that the rich, even though no more than a segment of the body politic, preserve its financial assets best, and that their superior intelligence makes them the best councillors; the main objection to oligarchy is, according to Athenagoras, that it gives the majority of citizens no share in profits but only in risks. As in the Old Oligarch, wealth and education are crucial factors for eligibility to office in oligarchies.

A unique definition of oligarchy is attributed by Thucydides to the Thebans' defense of their political system at the time of the Persian Wars. In their response to the Plataeans they declare that Thebes was at the time "neither an oligarchy based on a principle of political equality nor a democracy; affairs were controlled by a power-group of a few men (δυναστεία ὀλίγων ἀνδρῶν) , a system furthest removed from law and restraint but closest to a tyrant."[49] This means that, for purposes of their own, the Thebans distinguished between two kinds of oligarchy: they condemned a δυναστεία, a narrow régime in which eligibility to office was confined to a small circle of citizens, but approved, in addition to democracy, an oligarchy which recognized some kind of political equality (ὀλιγαρχία ἰσόνομος). No hint is given either in this speech or anywhere else in Thucydides what the "equal" kind of oligarchy might look like,[50] and oligarchy is

---

[47] Thuc. VI. 11. 7; on Spartan support of oligarchy, see I. 19. 1, III. 82. 1, IV. 74. 3–4; V. 31. 6, 81. 2.

[48] Id. VIII. 67. 3. All other provisions mentioned are so clearly linked to the situation at Athens at that time that no general conclusions on oligarchy can be drawn.

[49] Id. III. 62. 3: ἡμῖν μὲν γὰρ ἡ πόλις τότε ἐτύγχανεν οὔτε κατ᾽ ὀλιγαρχίαν ἰσόνομον πολιτεύουσα οὔτε κατὰ δημοκρατίαν· ὅπερ δέ ἐστι νόμοις μὲν καὶ τῷ σωφρονεστάτῳ ἐναντιώτατον, ἐγγυτάτω δὲ τυράννου, δυναστεία ὀλίγων ἀνδρῶν εἶχε τὰ πράγματα. Compare the appeal to ἰσονομία made by the democrats in Corcyra at III. 82. 8, as discussed above, pp. 21–22.

[50] For a discussion of this problem, see Ostwald (1969) 116–19.

never again discussed in these particular terms anywhere in Greek literature. Most noteworthy of all, this, to the best of my knowledge, is the only passage in extant classical Greek literature in which ὀλιγαρχία comes close to being praised as such; Megabyzus is described by Herodotus (III.81.1) as advocating ὀλιγαρχίη, but the speech attributed to him praises rule by the "best men" (III.81.3).

After the end of the fifth century democracy and oligarchy become little more than ideological footballs in party political conflicts, with the result that both tend to lose any significance as genuine principles in practical politics.[51] We find an early awareness of that in Peisander's self-serving arguments in Athens: after defining the oligarchy he wishes to introduce as "a different kind of democracy,"[52] he argues for its installation in terms which negate the importance of a principled ideology altogether: "we shall be deliberating in the present situation not so much about a régime as about our survival."[53]

Before we proceed to a discussion of the fourth century, it might be advisable to pause to consider what institutions were peculiar to oligarchies in the fifth century, i.e., before the end of the Peloponnesian War. The evidence is, unfortunately, very thin indeed. Even where we hear that a given state was an oligarchy, or that *stasis* changed its complexion from democracy to oligarchy – as in the cases of Corcyra or Megara, for example – we are usually given no more than the fact without any indication what institutions, if any, were involved. However much we hear about oligarchy in Megara – it had officials named πρόβουλοι in the 420s[54] – we do not learn what institutional changes the tightening of the oligarchy after Brasidas' conquest of the city brought with it.[55] We do not even know to what extent changes were mere changes in personnel rather than in institutions. The most explicit information on oligarchical institutions in the fifth century can be gleaned from the measures taken and projected in Athens in the oligarchical revolutions of 411 and 404 B.C.E. How typical it is of oligarchies in general we cannot tell.

---

[51] For a trenchant comparison of the oligarchical movements of 411 and 404 with those of 322 and 317 B.C.E., see Lehmann (1995).

[52] Thuc. VIII. 53. 1: μὴ τὸν αὐτὸν τρόπον δημοκρατουμένοις. Cf. 54. 1.

[53] Ibid. 53. 3: μὴ περὶ πολιτείας τὸ πλέον βουλεύσομεν ἐν τῷ παρόντι ἢ περὶ σωτηρίας.

[54] Ar., *Ach.* 755.

[55] Thuc. IV. 74. 4: καὶ ἐς ὀλιγαρχίαν τὰ μάλιστα κατέστησαν τὴν πόλιν. Similarly with the tightening of oligarchy in Sikyon in 417, see id. V. 81. 2, and the establishment of oligarchies among allied states in 411, see id. VIII. 64. 1–2.

The most universal feature is the restriction of the franchise and/or eligibility for office to a number of citizens, most broadly defined as "those most competent to render public service with their persons and their fortunes."[56] Their limit was set in Athens at five thousand in 411/10,[57] and at three thousand in 404.[58] Restrictions can be regarded as being further tightened in 404, when the Thirty abused their mandate to draft legislation by taking power into their own hands, and further still, when they appointed the Ten to succeed them.[59] That oligarchical rule was to be confined to the affluent is shown explicitly by the proposal at the Colonus meeting in 411 that all pay of public officials (except for archons and *prytaneis*) be suspended,[60] and implicitly by the fact that the revolt of 411 was fomented in Samos by the *trierarchs* and the most powerful men.[61] Wealth as a precondition for eligibility to office is also shown in the four Councils of the member states of the oligarchical Boeotian states at this time.[62] The four Boeotian councils presided in turn over plenary meetings of the League Council as a whole, but measures needed the assent of all four to be validated. It is quite likely that this became in Athens the pattern for the four sections (λήξεις) on which the election of the Council was to be based in the constitution framed "for the future" (*Ath.Pol.* 30. 3). The powers of the Council(s) in Athens were to be as absolute as they were in the Boeotian cities.[63] Moreover, the Athenian oligarchs made attendance at the meetings of the Council compulsory, on pain of a penalty of one drachma per day for meetings missed.[64] Finally, *probouloi*, ten of whom were instituted to meet the emergency situation after the Sicilian disaster in 413,[65] are consistently treated in Aristotle's *Politics* as an oligarchical institution.[66] We already remarked on their presence in – probably oligarchical – Megara.[67]

---

[56] I take this formulation from Arist., *Ath.Pol.* 29. 5 (τοῖς δυνατωτάτοις καὶ τοῖς σώμασιν καὶ τοῖς χρήμασιν λῃτουργεῖν), similarly in Thuc. VIII. 65. 3.

[57] Arist. *loc. cit.* ; Thuc. *loc. cit.* and 97. 1.

[58] Xen. *Hell.* II. 3. 18; Arist. *Ath. Pol.* 36. 1.

[59] In view of the confused and complex character of our sources, it is simplest to refer the reader to my discussion in Ostwald (1986) 475–90.

[60] Thuc. VIII. 65. 3, 67. 3; Arist. *Ath.Pol.* 29. 5, 30. 2.

[61] Thuc. ibid. 47. 2.

[62] See *Hell. Oxy.* (ed. Chambers, 1993) 19. 2.

[63] Thuc. VIII. 67. 3; Arist. *Ath. Pol.* 31. 1. For Boeotia, see the relation between βουλαί and Boeotarchs in 421 in Thuc. V. 38. 2–3.

[64] Arist. *Ath. Pol.* 29. 5; see also *Pol.* IV. 13, 1297a17–35, where the imposition of penalties for not attending meetings of the Assembly, and for avoiding jury-duty or military training are described as oligarchical.

[65] Arist. *Ath. Pol.* 29. 2 with Ostwald (1986) 338–43.

[66] Arist. *Pol.* IV. 14, 1298b29; 15, 1299b31–36; VI. 8, 1322b16, 1323a9.

[67] See n. 54 above.

There is no reason to assume that similar restrictions did not continue to characterize oligarchy in the fourth century and later.[68] But their substantive value was cheapened when its political and ideological usefulness was discovered in conflicts between rich and poor. About a decade after the end of the Peloponnesian War, soon after the restoration of the democracy, we find Lysias defending a client accused of having engaged in anti-democratic activities during the last years of the Peloponnesian War with the contention that "no human being exists who is by nature either an oligarch or a democrat, but whatever constitutional form brings him advantage he is eager to see established."[69] The speech attests not only the factiousness of Athenian society in this period, of which other sources give us more detailed information, but also the indifference of this particular citizen to any principled valuation of democracy and oligarchy. What democracy and oligarchy are is taken for granted; but both terms pale in significance before the more tangible criterion of the benefit an individual citizen can derive from it.

A passage in an address by Isocrates c. 370 B.C.E., written for delivery by the young Cypriote king Nicocles to his subjects, stands out in that it praises monarchy at the expense of both democracy and oligarchy. In applying the yardstick of what later came to be called "the two equalities,"[70] Isocrates condemns oligarchies and democracies alike for seeking to give equal status to those who are part of the system; the principle that no person should be entitled to have more than any other favors the worthless.[71] In contrast, monarchies distribute privileges in terms of merit: the greater the merit the higher the privilege conferred. "Even if this is not the established practice everywhere," Isocrates adds disarmingly, "this is the aim of this form of government."[72] The sincerity of these sentiments need

---

[68] For a brief but very useful discussion of oligarchy in the fourth-century orators, see Orsi (1981) esp. 135–38, 146–50.

[69] Lys. XXV. 8: πρῶτον μὲν οὖν ἐνθυμηθῆναι χρὴ ὅτι οὐδείς ἐστιν ἀνθρώπων φύσει οὔτε ὀλιγαρχικὸς οὔτε δημοκρατικός, ἀλλ' ἥτις ἂν ἑκάστῳ πολιτεία συμφέρῃ, ταύτην προθυμεῖται καθεστάναι. For a similar sentiment, see Isoc. VIII *De Pace* 133.

[70] Isoc. III *Nicocles* 14: ...οἶμαι πᾶσι δοκεῖν δεινότατον μὲν εἶναι τὸ τῶν αὐτῶν ἀξιοῦσθαι τοὺς χρηστοὺς καὶ τοὺς πονηρούς, δικαιότατον δὲ τὸ διωρίσθαι περὶ τούτων καὶ μὴ τοὺς ἀνομοίους τῶν ὁμοίων τυγχάνειν, ἀλλὰ καὶ πράττειν καὶ τιμᾶσθαι κατὰ τὴν ἀξίαν ἑκάστους.

[71] Ibid. 15: αἱ μὲν τοίνυν ὀλιγαρχίαι καὶ δημοκρατίαι τὰς ἰσότητας τοῖς μετέχουσι τῶν πολιτειῶν ζητοῦσι, καὶ τοῦτ' εὐδοκιμεῖ παρ' αὐταῖς, ἢν μηδὲν ἕτερος ἑτέρου δύνηται πλέον ἔχειν· ὃ τοῖς πονηροῖς συμφέρον ἐστίν.

[72] Ibid.: αἱ δὲ μοναρχίαι πλεῖστον μὲν νέμουσι τῷ βελτίστῳ, δεύτερον δὲ τῷ μετ' ἐκεῖνον, τρίτον δὲ καὶ τέταρτον τοῖς ἄλλοις κατὰ τὸν αὐτὸν λόγον. καὶ ταῦτ' εἰ μὴ πανταχοῦ καθέστηκεν, ἀλλὰ τό γε βούλημα τῆς πολιτείας τοιοῦτόν ἐστιν.

not concern us here. But it is extraordinary to see the principle of "arithmetic" equality extended to oligarchies for no apparent reason other than putting into high relief the claim of monarchy to be the sole proponent of "geometrical" equality. Further, since in this particular tract Isocrates does not differentiate between tyrant (τυρανν-) and king (βασιλ-), his purpose in using the more neutral μοναρχ-stem seems to be to avoid overt praise of tyranny as the most equitable rule: after all, though Isocrates does not use the term ἀριστοκρατία here, he treats "monarchy" in the *Nicocles* as the rule of the best; if he had had our vocabulary available, he would probably have called it "meritocracy."[73]

The term ἀριστοκρατία, which has an ironic twist in Thucydides,[74] vanishes completely in the fourth century from the vocabulary of the orators. Moreover, neither Aeschines and Demosthenes make any reference to kingship (βασιλεύς, βασιλεία) as a form of government; "kings" appear only as titles of actual monarchs (of Persia, Thrace, Macedonia, et al.).[75] Aeschines recognizes tyranny, oligarchy, and democracy as governments by one, a few, and many, respectively; but there is no attempt either in his writings or in Demosthenes' to evaluate them dispassionately. Tyranny is always a despicable perversion of any form of government, and oligarchy is often bracketed with it; both are run by the whims of those who control them.[76] Democracy is invariably the polar opposite of oligarchy for both Aeschines and Demosthenes, but we learn next to nothing about the institutions or structure of either: democracy is credited with all social goods, especially freedom, while oligarchy embodies all evils.[77] This attitude is

---

[73] Cf. also id. XII *Panath.* 132, where μοναρχία is used in place of τυραννίς, to make the point that any constitution can be an ἀριστοκρατία, if it is well run. On this problem, see also Too (1995) 103–4.

[74] See above, p. 22 with n. 42.

[75] The sole exception is the metaphorical description of the individual as "king" in a democracy at Aeschin. III *Ctes.* 233: ἀνὴρ γὰρ ἰδιώτης ἐν πόλει δημοκρατουμένῃ νόμῳ καὶ ψήφῳ βασιλεύει.

[76] Aeschin. I *Tim.* 4–5, III *Ctes.* 6; Dem. XIX *Falsa Leg.* 184, XX *Lept.* 15, XXIV *Tim.* 149.

[77] To give a complete list would be tedious and unnecessary. Some examples will suffice: **democracy** is law-abiding (Aeschin. I *Tim.* 4–5, Dem. XXIV *Timocr.* 76), based on equality (Aeschin. I *Tim.* 5), its citizen is sensible (Aeschin. III *Ctes.* 168), anyone can address the people (Aeschin. III *Ctes.* 220), it enjoys freedom and constitutional government (Dem. XV *Rhod.* 17 and 19), and it has a pleasant lifestyle (Dem. XXII *Androt.* 51). **Oligarchy** is governed by the whim of the rulers (Aeschin. I *Tim.* 4, Dem. XXIV *Timocr.* 76), it is an armed camp full of suspicion (Aeschin. I *Tim.* 5), based on inequality (Aeschin. I *Tim.* 5), the individual is worthless and has all bad qualities (Aeschin. III *Ctes.* 169 and 170), only the powerful can address the people (Aeschin. III *Ctes.* 220, Dem. XV *Rhod.* 18; XXII *Androt.* 32), it is an enemy of freedom and treats its people like slaves (Dem. XV *Rhod.* 19 and 21; XXIV *Timocr.* 75), and it is brutish and violent (Dem. XXIV *Timocr.* 75).

almost certainly a residual effect of the Athenian experiences of 411 and 404 and the enmities they generated. That régimes are run for the benefit of the ruling element under each constitution is taken for granted. The names by which the régimes are known have degenerated into tendentious party-political tags, from which nothing can be learned about the true nature of either democracy or oligarchy.

3. PHILOSOPHICAL REVALUATION: PLATO

ἀριστοκρατία makes a startling reappearance in Plato's *Republic*. He has Socrates take as his point of departure Thrasymachus' conventional tripartite classification of constitutions into tyranny, democracy, and aristocracy as typefying his contention that the laws in each constitution reflect the advantage of the ruling element.[78] That under these circumstances a tyrant rather than a king or monarch should represent the rule of one makes good sense, because tyrannical rule was regarded by definition as benefitting only the ruler. What is somewhat harder to understand is why aristocracy rather than oligarchy represents government of a few. Considering that ἀριστοκρατία had fallen out of fashion among his contemporaries, Plato's purpose may have been to revive the term and infuse it with a new, more literal meaning: by pointing out through Thrasymachus that even under the "rule of the best" the laws articulate the advantage of the ruling element alone, he may have wished to demonstrate the inadequacy of the conventional tripartite classification. In his opinion, none of the governments in the world in which we live pursues the true goal of governance, the "real" good of the governed.[79] This "real" good cannot be ascertained by looking at actual states, but by discovering a transcendental model of "justice" in light of which human societies ought to be run.

The break with the conventional tripartite scheme is abruptly announced at the end of *Republic* IV, but a fuller discussion is deferred until the opening of Book VIII. With justice in both the individual and in the state as his criterion, Socrates unexpectedly asserts that there are five different types of individuals as well as of states, one characterized as excellent and four as inferior; he proposes to call the excellent state "'kingship' (βασιλεία) if one outstanding man arises among its rulers, and 'rule of the best' (ἀριστοκρατία) if more than one."[80] In this, his first response to Thrasymachus, an "aristocracy" is not the rule of a few best men governing in their own interest, but government by those who can realize transcendental justice in human society.

---

[78] Pl., *Resp.* I. 338d7–8: τῶν πόλεων αἱ μὲν τυραννοῦνται, αἱ δὲ δημοκρατοῦνται, αἱ δὲ ἀριστοκρατοῦνται.

[79] See Pl., *Ep.* VII. 326a–b.

[80] Pl., *Resp.* IV. 444e–445e, esp. 445d6–7: ἐγγενομένου μὲν γὰρ ἀνδρὸς ἑνὸς ἐν τοῖς ἄρχουσι διαφέροντος βασιλεία ἂν κληθείη, πλειόνων δὲ ἀριστοκρατία.

The argument, interrupted at this point by the request of his interlocutors to hear more about the place of women and children as held in common by all Guardians, is left in abeyance until the opening of Book VIII. There, after a final reference to the status of women and children, Socrates returns to a detailed statement of the (now) five types of constitution and of the individuals dominating each. The connection with Book IV is established by referring to the only good type as ἀριστοκρατία (544e7), and by identifying the four inferior types of states and individuals as, respectively, timocracy, oligarchy, democracy, and tyranny (VIII. 544c1–IX. 588a11). In short, the purpose of Plato's ranking is to show the degree to which actual states are removed from the best. Oligarchy in his scheme follows a constitution which had not previously entered Greek political discussion, "timocracy," the kind of government enjoyed by Sparta and Crete, in which the military virtues of competition and love of honour characterize the ethos of the state.[81] Oligarchy develops from a backlash against the suppressive puritanical régime of timocracy and results in the institution of private property and its concomitant craving for wealth, which divides the state into rich and poor and puts the reins of government into the hand of the "few" rich; in short, "oligarchy" is marked by the pursuit of wealth.[82] Only the misrule of the uneducated and undisciplined masses, "democracy," and the terror spread by the régime of a "tyrant" are worse. The reasons for the division of the rule of the few into two are likely to be found in Plato's assessment of the régime of the Thirty: they had started out with a genuine desire to reform the state after the misrule of the democracy, but had soon let their greed and rapaciousness deteriorate it from "timocracy" into "oligarchy".[83]

Plato did not intend to be rigid about his scheme or inflexible about the number of types;[84] his chief concern here seems to have been to demonstrate the irrelevance of the conventional constitutional forms in relation to philosophical rule. The scheme of the *Republic* was not to be Plato's last word on the classification of constitutions. Incipient doubts that a sufficiently large number of experts could ever be found to rule the paradigmatic state are reflected already in the *Republic* in that he modified his views of "scientific" government from the ἀριστοκρατία of the Guardians to the

---

[81] Pl., *Resp.* VIII. 545c8–548d5.

[82] Ibid. 550c8–555b2.

[83] Pl., *Ep.* VII. 324b–325c.

[84] See ibid. VIII. 544d1–4: δυναστεῖαι γὰρ καὶ ὠνηταὶ βασιλεῖαι καὶ τοιαῦταί τινες πολιτεῖαι μεταξύ τι τούτων πού εἰσιν, εὕροι δ' ἄν τις αὐτὰς οὐκ ἐλάττους περὶ τοὺς βαρβάρους ἢ τοὺς Ἕλληνας. Note also that he uses τιμαρχία without distinction from τιμοκρατία at 545b7 and 550d3.

βασιλεία of the Philosopher.⁸⁵ Advancing years further increased his doubts about the power of education to perfect human nature. The *Statesman* begins by establishing as the good ruler no longer a metaphysician but a managerial expert, a royal πολιτικός rather than a Philosopher-king; it ends by despairing of the feasibility of finding even a political expert to rule existing states, and proposes as a second best (δεύτερος πλοῦς, 301c1–3) a new criterion for ranking states, on the basis of the conventional tripartite division, into six types.⁸⁶

Return from the rule of an expert to a tripartite division can be read as indicating that non-transcendental everyday actualities forced their attention on Plato; but that is not the full story. He still rejects the conventional views that good government depends on the rule of one, of a few, or of the many; on whether the rulers are wealthy or poor; on whether they rule violently or with the consent of the governed; or on whether they use or do not use written laws (292a5–8). As his own criterion he proposes a government informed by the expert knowledge (ἐπιστήμη) of the royal statesman (βασιλικός) (292c5–293a1). Since the rule of such a person is not realizable here on earth, his régime is placed in a category by itself,⁸⁷ and the remaining constitutions are classified into six in accordance with the degree to which each emulates or fails to emulate the rule of the political expert, expressed in adherence to or rejection of written laws which embody his precepts (291d-301a). Thus, Plato distinguishes three law-abiding and three law-flouting constitutions: monarchy is differentiated into kingship and tyranny, the rule of a few into aristocracy and oligarchy, and the rule of the many into two kinds of democracy which, respectively, observe or transgress the laws.⁸⁸ Of these six forms, kingship is the best and tyranny the worst; aristocracy is second and oligarchy fifth; while democracy is at once "the worst of the genuine, law-abiding constitutions, and the best of all those that transgress the laws."⁸⁹ What had been ἀριστοκρατία in the *Republic*, is here confined to the unrealizable rule of one man; ἀριστοκρα-

---

⁸⁵ See Ostwald (1971).

⁸⁶ On the *Statesman* as a "bridge between the utopian and anti-democratic *Republic*, on the one hand, and the more compromising mood of the *Laws* on the other" see Rowe (1995a) 14–19, esp 17; cf. also Kahn (1995).

⁸⁷ Pl., *Plt.* 302e4–8, cf. 301d8–e4: νῦν δέ γε ὁπότε οὐκ ἔστι γιγνόμενος, ὡς δή φαμεν, ἐν ταῖς πόλεσι βασιλεὺς οἷος ἐν σμήνεσιν ἐμφύεται, τό τε σῶμα εὐθὺς καὶ τὴν ψυχὴν διαφέρων εἷς, δεῖ δὴ συνελθόντες συγγράμματα γράφειν, ὡς ἔοικεν, μεταθέοντας τὰ τῆς ἀληθεστάτης πολιτείας ἴχνη.

⁸⁸ Ibid. 302e1–2: τό γε κατὰ νόμους ἄρχειν καὶ παρανόμως.

⁸⁹ Ibid. 303a7–8: διὸ γέγονε πασῶν μὲν νομίμων τῶν πολιτειῶν οὐσῶν τούτων χειρίστη, παρανόμων δὲ οὐσῶν συμπασῶν βελτίστη.

τία is paired in the *Statesman* with ὀλιγαρχία as the good rule of a few, but, like ὀλιγαρχία in the *Republic,* it is characterized as a rule of the rich.[90]

There is no new classification or valuation of constitutions in Plato's last work on political theory, the *Laws,* because Plato is so intent upon establishing his Cretan colony on a radically new basis of government by law that he rejects all existing forms of government alike as "non-constitutions" and "faction-states," remaining completely indifferent to their number and their differentiae.[91] Only when in Book IV the issue becomes how good constitutional legislation can best be implemented do existing constitutional forms become relevant. Plato argues that a young tyrant, endowed with a retentive memory, quick intelligence, courage, and a natural authority can create good government most effectively, next two such men, and progressively more men less efficiently: "the easiest step is from a tyranny, the second from constitutional kingship, the third from some kind of democracy. The fourth, oligarchy, is equipped to produce a state of this sort only with the greatest difficulty, since it engenders the largest number of powerful men."[92] It is not surprising that aristocracy has no place in this context.[93] The division of the rule of one into tyranny and constitutional kingship with the priority being given to tyranny occasions some surprise; but it is easily explained by reference to the licence given the royal expert in the *Statesman* (293d4–e5) to kill and send into exile intransigeant citizens for the good of the state: a new order is more easily initiated by one whose authority does not require the consent of the governed than by a constitutional king whose authority does require it. The superiority of democracy over oligarchy, on the other hand, rests on the assumption that any actual democracy is dominated by a smaller number of leaders than an oligarchy. In short, the tripartite division shows that the *Laws,* too, gives no serious consideration to actual constitutions; when referring to them it uses the

---

[90] Ibid. 301a6–8: ὅταν ἄρα οἱ πλούσιοι ταύτην μιμοῦνται, τότε ἀριστοκρατίαν καλοῦμεν τὴν τοιαύτην πολιτείαν· ὁπόταν δὲ τῶν νόμων μὴ φροντίζωσιν, ὀλιγαρχίαν.

[91] See esp. Pl., *Lg.* VIII. 832b10–c3: τὰς οὐ πολιτείας ἔγωγε αἰτίας εἶναί φημι ἃς πολλάκις εἴρηκα ἐν τοῖς πρόσθεν λόγοις, δημοκρατίαν καὶ ὀλιγαρχίαν καὶ τυραννίδα. τούτων γὰρ δὴ πολιτεία μὲν οὐδεμία, στασιωτεῖαι δὲ πᾶσαι λέγοιντ' ἂν ὀρθότατα. Cf. also IV. 712b8–c5 with e9–713a2, where democracy, oligarchy, aristocracy, kingship, and tyranny are called non-constitutions.

[92] Ibid. IV. 710e3–7: ... ἀλλ' ἐκ τυραννίδος μὲν πρῶτον, δεύτερον δὲ ἐκ βασιλικῆς πολιτείας, τρίτον δὲ ἔκ τινος δημοκρατίας. τὸ δὲ τέταρτον, ὀλιγαρχία, τὴν τοῦ τοιούτου γένεσιν χαλεπώτατα δύναιτ' ἂν προσδέξασθαι· πλεῖστοι γὰρ ἐν αὐτῇ δυνάσται γίγνονται.

[93] It is only mentioned when, in the immediate sequel at 712c3–5, the question about the "best constitution" for the new colony is brought up.

conventional tripartite classification with only insignificant variations. The work advocates a régime informed by laws formulated along philosophical lines by the best experts available; it remains indifferent to conventional systems of government, including oligarchy. The criterion for evaluation remains what it had been toward the end of the *Statesman*.

4. THEORY AND PRACTICE: ARISTOTLE

With Aristotle we come to the most profound and wide-ranging political thinker of all classical antiquity. He is the first serious systematic student of politics in that he blended the theoretical concerns he had absorbed as a student of Plato with astute observation of historical realities. This comes out in what is probably his earliest classification of constitutions in the *Rhetoric*. Persuasiveness and good advice, he argues, depend on a speaker's knowledge of the political system under which his audience is living. The nature of a political system is determined by who is in charge of it. On this basis he identifies four[94] kinds of constitution and states the goal of each: in a democracy, offices are assigned by lot and its aim is freedom; oligarchies base eligibility on property qualifications, and their aim is wealth; aristocracies appoint men to office on the basis of their education, which is specified by law, and whose aim is the maintenance of this education and its institutions; and monarchy, the rule of one, is subdivided into orderly constitutional kingship and unregulated tyranny, whose aim is its own protection.[95] There is no transcendent principle or theory here. Aristotle is indifferent to the number of constitutional systems; each system is empirically identified in terms of the authority actually ruling and the values actually prevailing in each. The scheme is designed to meet the practical needs of the *Rhetoric*, not to lay the foundations for a political theory. Aristotle does not revert to it anywhere in his later works.

Historical reality is mixed with theory in Aristotle's best-known and most fundamental classification of constitutions. The scheme found in the *Politics*[96] is clearly based on – or at least influenced by – Plato's "second

---

[94] Strictly speaking, the division of μοναρχία into βασιλεία and τυραννίς results in five kinds.

[95] Arist., *Rhet*. I. 8, 1365b21–1366a16, esp. 1365b31–1366a6: ἔστιν δὲ δημοκρατία μὲν πολιτεία ἐν ᾗ κλήρῳ διανέμονται τὰς ἀρχάς, ὀλιγαρχία δὲ ἐν ᾗ οἱ ἀπὸ τιμημάτων, ἀριστοκρατία δὲ ἐν ᾗ κατὰ τὴν παιδείαν· παιδείαν δὲ λέγω τὴν ὑπὸ τοῦ νόμου κειμένην....ἔστι δὲ δημοκρατίας μὲν τέλος ἐλευθερία, ὀλιγαρχίας δὲ πλοῦτος, ἀριστοκρατίας δὲ τὰ περὶ παιδείαν καὶ τὰ νόμιμα, τυραννίδος δὲ φυλακή.

[96] I exclude from consideration here Aristotle's discussion of the "best constitution" (ἀρίστη πολιτεία) in *Politics* VII, because it is "the absolutely best, and not the best which is 'possible in the circumstances of the case'" (Barker [1948] 279 n. 2), and thus not germane to a discussion of oligarchy. See also Schütrumpf (1980) 1–66.

best" scheme in the *Statesman*,[97] that is, a rule based not on the guidance of a "royal" expert, but on obedience to law. Like Plato, Aristotle begins with a tripartite division of "good" constitutions and opposes to each a "bad" perversion, but unlike Plato he does not oppose them to the unattainable rule of a royal expert. Further, Aristotle does not dismiss all existing states as flawed; instead of using as his criterion the degree to which each adheres to or flouts the (written) laws that emulate the expert's rule, he adopts a more pragmatic criterion: whether the ruling element governs to promote its own interest or the interest of the governed.

This is a powerful response to Thrasymachus' argument in the *Republic*: Thrasymachus had envisaged the interest of the rulers as the only possible aim of government. Aristotle follows Plato in rejecting the interest of the rulers as a valid criterion; but instead of looking toward abstract principles to inform good government, he envisages an alternative to Thrasymachus: he believes that it is possible to find rulers capable of discovering what is good for the governed and implement it rather than exploit the governed for their own profit. What "the good of the governed" is he does not attempt to state: it cannot be articulated as a set of abstract principles, such as Plato's "Good," outside the field of common experience. Aristotle's absolutes are found pragmatically embedded in the world in which we live and in which we have to act; they are "correct," "good for a given purpose" rather than "Good" as such. The "correct" (ὀρθαί) forms of government are those which have the welfare of the governed at heart; those who aim at what is good for the rulers are "deviations" (παρεκβάσεις). The "correct" forms are in descending order of goodness kingship, aristocracy, and polity (πολιτεία); the "deviations" are, in descending order of "badness," tyranny, oligarchy, and democracy. What remains Platonic is the recognition of an absolute value of "correctness" measured against which the incorrect is a "deviation." What makes "correctness" "correct" is not made explicit, but it is more likely to be ascertained by empirical than by theoretical means.

Aristotle's pragmatic bent results in his identification of an unprecedented and new form of government, which he dubs πολιτεία, and which, formally, takes the place of Plato's law-abiding democracy. It is a kind of "mixed" constitution, usually transliterated as "polity" in English rather than translated, in order to avoid confusion with other connotations attached to *politeia* in Aristotle and in Greek writers in general ("constitution," "citizenship," "political order," etc.).[98] Aristotle explains its meaning in *Politics* IV, chapters 8 and 9, as a thorough blend of oligarchical and

---

[97] Compare Arist., *Pol*. III. 7, 1279a22–b10 with Pl. *Plt*. 297c–303b and pp. 33–34 above.

[98] For a comprehensive study, see Bordes (1982).

democratic principles, in which affluence and indigence, wealth, and freedom are reconciled with one another, and in which the rich are identical with the social élite (καλοὶ κἀγαθοί) (1293b33–34, 1294a15–23).[99] In judicial matters, an oligarchical principle of penalizing the well-to-do who try to shirk jury duty exists side by side with the democratic pay for jury duty, in order to enable the indigent to participate in the judicial process; property qualification for citizenship is kept low, and magistrates are appointed by vote (not by lot), but eligibility to office does not depend on property qualifications (1294a30–b13). He sums up his definition: "A well-mixed polity must palpably contain features of oligarchy as well as of democracy – and of neither. It should depend on itself for its survival and not on external support, and its internal support should not be contingent on a majority desiring its survival – for that could also be the case in a bad constitution – but on no single segment of the city even desiring to have a different constitution."[100]

Thus Aristotle's "polity" becomes not merely a substitute for Plato's "law-abiding democracy." Like Plato's "royal expert," it becomes also the best of the forms of government that envisages the good of the governed: knowledge of abstract eternally true principles implemented by a single ruler gives way to practical considerations which empirically blend economic, social, and political factors into a cohesive society.

Pragmatic considerations are evident also when in *Nicomachean Ethics* VIII Aristotle applies a similar pattern to φιλία ("friendship") in political relations. While retaining the terms "kingship" and "aristocracy" for good government of one and of a few, respectively, he uses "timocracy" (τιμοκρατία) as an alternate name for what he calls "polity" in the *Politics,* defining it as a constitution based on property qualifications (ἀπὸ τιμημάτων).[101] Plato had applied this term to an oligarchy of the Laconian and Cretan type (*Resp.* VIII. 544c–545a), because the quest for honor dominates them (τιμή); Aristotle, who had included the Laconian constitution in his own definition of "polity" at *Politics* IV. 9, 1294b19, derives the term in the *Nicomachean Ethics* from τίμημα ("property qualification"), thus giving it an oligarchical twist, since ownership of property is for him one of the hallmarks of oligarchy.[102] In replacing Plato's "good" democracy with

---

[99] For an explanation of these terms, see ch. 5 (d) below, pp. 52–68.

[100] Arist., *Pol.* IV. 9, 1294b34–40: δεῖ δ᾽ ἐν τῇ πολιτείᾳ τῇ μεμειγμένῃ καλῶς ἀμφότερα δοκεῖν εἶναι καὶ μηδέτερον, καὶ σώζεσθαι δι᾽ αὑτῆς καὶ μὴ ἔξωθεν, καὶ δι᾽ αὑτῆς μὴ τῷ πλείους [ἔξωθεν] εἶναι τοὺς βουλομένους (εἴη γὰρ ἂν καὶ πονηρᾷ πολιτείᾳ τοῦθ᾽ ὑπάρχον) ἀλλὰ τῷ μηδ᾽ ἂν βούλεσθαι πολιτείαν ἑτέραν μηθὲν τῶν τῆς πόλεως μορίων ὅλως.

[101] Arist., *EN* VIII. 10, 1160a31–b22.

[102] See Arist., *Pol.* IV. 9, 1294b10, V. 6, 1306b8–9. See also below, ch. 5 (b).

"timocracy," Aristotle now ties timocracy more closely to democracy: "timocracy, too, tends to encompass the majority in that all those who meet a given property qualification are equal."[103]

We shall have occasion to return to this passage later. For the moment it will suffice to underline the importance of property in citizenship in a "good" society, even in a form of democracy. For Plato possession of personal property had such a great potential for being detrimental to the state that he prohibited it for the Guardians; it comes to play a role in the constitutional structure of the state only when it degenerates from a "timocracy" into an oligarchy.[104] For Aristotle in the *Nicomachean Ethics*, the emergence of property qualifications is set at the change from aristocracy to the "good" form of oligarchy; that is, it enters with the onset of moral indifference (κακία) to merit on the part of the aristocratic rulers in the distribution of offices and honors; it occurs when they keep all or most of the good jobs to themselves, assign always the same people to offices, and give highest priority to the accumulation of wealth; rule of a few immoral men will replace the most decent rulers (1160b12–16). "Property" has a positive prefix in Aristotle's timocracy.

---

[103] Arist., *EN* VIII. 10, 1160b17–19: ἐκ δὲ τιμοκρατίας εἰς δημοκρατίαν· σύνοροι γὰρ εἰσιν αὗται· πλήθους γὰρ βούλεται καὶ ἡ τιμοκρατία εἶναι, καὶ ἴσοι πάντες οἱ ἐν τῷ τιμήματι.

[104] Pl., *Resp.* VIII. 550c–551c with n. 82 above.

5. THE OLIGARCHICAL CITIZEN IN ARISTOTLE

A. THE PLACE OF OLIGARCHY

Aristotle's empirical treatment of oligarchy stands at the end of a historical process in the course of which it became the antithesis to democracy, not on grounds of intrinsic merit but in the wake of the development of political ideologies. In attempting to infuse substance and meaning into constitutional ideologies, his contribution to the definition and classification of constitutions establishes a landmark in our understanding of government of a few.[105]

For Aristotle's contribution to the theory and practice of the rule of a few we must look to the *Politics*. The structure of that work prevents him from confining a discussion of its various aspects to one particular section of the work. Rather, we find it scattered over different books among the treatment of major general themes:[106] Book III, chapters 9–13, treats questions of citizenship, constitutional structure, and distributive justice in oligarchies; Book IV, chapters 3–10, outlines the varieties of government of a few, and chapters 14–16 the distribution of executive, deliberative, and judicial powers; Book V, chapters 5–12, deals with revolutions and changes from one form of government into another; and Book VI, chapters 6–8, discusses the construction of oligarchies. In addition, relevant remarks may appear incidentally in practically any part of the *Politics*. A wide-ranging discussion of this sort, different parts of which were almost certainly composed at different periods in Aristotle's life,[107] is not conducive to a consistent and uniform picture of oligarchy. Yet, this said, Aristotle's views on oligarchy remain remarkably consistent, and apparent inconsistencies can often be explained as due to changing perspectives required by the contexts in which oligarchy is discussed.[108]

---

[105] Whibley (1896), the classic study in English on the subject, is based almost exclusively on Aristotle.

[106] The following is based on the table of contents of Barker (1948), vii–ix, which provides the most useful overview of the work. For a different order of Aristotle's arrangement, see Simpson (1998) xiii–xxxvi.

[107] For an excellent survey down to 1960 of various theories of composition, see Weil (1960) 25–84; for a concise statement of more recent scholarly views, see Lord (1984) 14–17.

[108] On the unity of the *Politics*, see the sensible discussion of Simpson (1998) xvi–xx.

5. The Oligarchical Citizen in Aristotle

In defining various kinds of constitution, Aristotle tries to get away from the quantitative differentiae of government by one, by a few, and by the many, which had characterized conventional thinking. His analysis is based more on the constituent parts of society that dominate a given form of government.[109] As constituent parts he names kinship groups (οἰκίαι), economic groups (well-to-do, indigent, intermediate), which become in military terms hoplites and non-hoplites, occupational groups found among the common people (agricultural, commercial, and industrial), and among the upper classes differences in wealth and size of estates and in birth and achievements.[110] The form of government prevalent in a given state depends on which of these groups – or combination of groups – dominates its social structure: "for a constitution is the structure of public offices," Aristotle continues; "all states assign offices either in terms of the influence a given element enjoys among the members of the state, or in terms of some equality all members share: I mean, for example, the influence of the indigent or the well-to-do, or an equality common to both."[111]

Even though Aristotle does not explicitly say so, it is clear that this statement is not likely to apply to the two kinds of rule by one, kingship and tyranny, since in them there is no distribution of offices among the members of the state. But Aristotle regards as too simplistic the general view that only democracy and oligarchy are derived from these constituent parts, and that aristocracy is a kind of oligarchy and polity a kind of democracy (1290a13–18): "our classification is closer to the truth and better: there are two (or one) well-constructed constitutions" – he means kingship and aristocracy (1289a38–b5) – "and the rest are deviations, partly from a well-integrated mixture, partly from the best constitution; oligarchical when they are stricter and more autocratic, populist when they are relaxed and

---

[109] The dominating group as a whole is called πολίτευμα (= "governing body") at *Pol.* III. 6, 1278b11 and 7, 1279a25–31, where it is discussed in the wider terms of government by one, few, and many.

[110] Arist., *Pol.* IV. 3, 1289b27–1290a5.

[111] Ibid. 1290a7–11: πολιτεία μὲν γὰρ ἡ τῶν ἀρχῶν τάξις ἐστί, ταύτας δὲ διανέμονται πάντες ἢ κατὰ τὴν δύναμιν τῶν μετεχόντων ἢ κατά τιν' αὐτῶν ἰσότητα κοινήν, λέγω δ' οἷον τῶν ἀπόρων ἢ τῶν εὐπόρων ἢ κοινήν τιν' ἀμφοῖν. It is difficult to decide whether the κοινήν of the last phrase refers to the preceding δύναμιν or ἰσότητα. Although Newman (1902) 55, and Aubonnet (1971)149 with 298 n. 4, favor the former, I prefer, with Rackham (1944) 287, the latter, because it conforms more closely with the structure of the sentence as a whole. The meaning seems to be that in some states access to public office is open to citizens (μετεχόντων) on the basis of the influence the element dominating society has; in other states criteria that do not differentiate citizens from one another determine eligibility to office, among which, I presume, are legitimate birth, membership in a tribe, family, or a religious group. For the various qualitative and quantitative constituents of a group, see IV. 12, 1296b13–34.

a. The place of oligarchy

gentle."[112] This is the broadest as well as vaguest definition of oligarchy in Aristotle: oligarchy is a deviation from or perversion of aristocracy (cf. also III. 7, 1279b5); its main differentia from democracy is that it rules with a tighter rein. The reason is evidently that the ruling element is recruited from a narrower circle in an oligarchy than it is in a democracy.

We are faced here with a fairly radical departure from the conventional quantitative standard: democracy is not just government by the many and oligarchy not just government by the few. As stated at the opening of *Politics* IV. 4: "One should not assume, as some people do nowadays, that democracy is no more than a régime in which the majority has the final authority, for it is true also in oligarchies and everywhere that authority rests with the greater number; nor should one assume that oligarchy is a régime where a few have authority over the state. For if, of a given total of thirteen hundred, one thousand were wealthy, and if these were to make ineligible for office the three hundred poor despite the fact that they are free and like them in all other respects, no one would say that their government is a democracy. Similarly, if a few poor men had power over a majority of the well-to-do, no one would call a state like that an oligarchy, either, if, despite their wealth, the rest had no share in prestigious office. Rather, we must say that popular government exists when authority rests in the hands of free men, and oligarchy when authority rests in the hands of the wealthy: that the former are many and the latter few is only accidental, for many are free but few are wealthy."[113] Oligarchy, in short, is not the rule of a minority but the rule of the wealthy.

---

[112] Ibid. 1290a24–29: ἀληθέστερον δὲ καὶ βέλτιον ὡς ἡμεῖς διείλομεν, δυοῖν ἢ μιᾶς οὔσης τῆς καλῶς συνεστηκυίας τὰς ἄλλας εἶναι παρεκβάσεις. τὰς μὲν τῆς εὖ κεκραμμένης ἁρμονίας τὰς δὲ τῆς ἀρίστης πολιτείας, ὀλιγαρχικὰς μὲν τὰς συντονωτέρας καὶ δεσποτικωτέρας, τὰς δ' ἀνειμένας καὶ μαλακὰς δημοτικάς. Newman (1902) 157 remarks ad loc. that, whereas at 1289a38–b9 oligarchy, democracy, and tyranny are deviations, "Aristotle...speaks in the passage before us as if the polity was also a deviation-form, but this is probably by inadvertence; he speaks more exactly in c. 8. 1293b23 sqq."

[113] Arist., *Pol.* IV. 4, 1290a30–b3: Οὐ δεῖ δὲ τιθέναι δημοκρατίαν, καθάπερ εἰώθασί τινες νῦν, ὅπου κύριον τὸ πλῆθος (καὶ γὰρ ἐν ταῖς ὀλιγαρχίαις καὶ πανταχοῦ τὸ πλέον μέρος κύριον), οὐδ' ὀλιγαρχίαν, ὅπου κύριοι ὀλίγοι τῆς πολιτείας. εἰ γὰρ εἴησαν οἱ πάντες χίλιοι καὶ τριακόσιοι, καὶ τούτων οἱ χίλιοι πλούσιοι, καὶ μὴ μεταδιδοῖεν ἀρχῆς τοῖς τριακοσίοις καὶ πένησιν ἐλευθέροις οὖσι καὶ τἆλλα ὁμοίως, οὐδεὶς ἂν φαίη δημοκρατεῖσθαι τούτους· ὁμοίως δὲ καὶ εἰ πένητες ὀλίγοι μὲν εἶεν, κρείττους δὲ τῶν εὐπόρων πλειόνων ὄντων, οὐδεὶς ἂν ὀλιγαρχίαν προσαγορεύσειεν οὐδὲ τὴν τοιαύτην, εἰ τοῖς ἄλλοις οὖσι πλουσίοις μὴ μετείη τῶν τιμῶν. μᾶλλον τοίνυν λεκτέον ὅτι δῆμος μέν ἐστιν ὅταν οἱ ἐλεύθεροι κύριοι ὦσιν, ὀλιγαρχία δ' ὅταν οἱ πλούσιοι, ἀλλὰ συμβαίνει τοὺς μὲν πολλοὺς εἶναι τοὺς δ' ὀλίγους· ἐλεύθεροι μὲν γὰρ πολλοί, πλούσιοι δ' ὀλίγοι. Cf. III. 8, 1279b20–26 and IV. 8, 1294a11–14.

The statement that oligarchy is characterized as the rule of the wealthy is not as intelligible as it might appear at a first glance, primarily because modern translators of Aristotle have been as indifferent as commentators have been to the facts that (a) Aristotle uses several different notions of what we call "property" and that (b) he has two sets of expressions, εὔπορος-ἄπορος and πλούσιος-πένης and their cognate nouns and verbs, to differentiate economically advantaged and disadvantaged classes from one another. We have chosen "well-to-do"-"indigent" and "wealthy"-"poor" to retain this difference. Yet while the latter pair accurately reflects the sense of the Greek, there is no adequate English rendering of εὔπορος-ἄπορος, which is much more vital for an understanding of Aristotle's political thought, especially on oligarchy. Accordingly, we have to examine the significance of property and its valuation, and especially the meaning of wealth before concentrating on the varieties of oligarchy and their distinction from one another.

B. PROPERTY AND CITIZENSHIP

In the absence of regular pay for public service in the Greek city-states, a minimum of εὐπορία was needed for the full enjoyment of citizenship, since citizenship involved giving freely of one's time and service to the community. This required ownership of property not only in oligarchies but also in democracies,[114] and we must at this point inquire what the relation of citizenship to "property" was for the Greeks. In stating that no State shall "deprive any person of life, liberty, and property without due process of law," the Fourteenth Amendment to the Constitution of the United States guarantees to all, citizen and non-citizen alike,[115] the inviolability of their property: no one can be deprived of it "without due process of law;" the legitimate ownership of property is a right to which all, citizen and non-citizen, are entitled. This was not the view of the ancient Greeks. Ownership of property, especially real property, was not a right enjoyed by all, but was restricted in most states to citizens, and was more usually than not a prerequisite for participation in the political process. This need not be surprising: even in more recent times political systems have been based on the conviction that a person of property has a greater "stake in the country" than a poor person. Since he stands more to lose in case of a common emergency, the argument goes, his opinions should carry greater weight in shaping political decisions and in managing public affairs. Although, as we

---

[114] Arist., *Pol.* III. 8, 1279b17–19; VII. 9, 1329a18–21. See above, p. 40.
[115] See the discussion of Amar (1998) 170–74 with n. 42.

learn from Aristotle, this belief was indeed held in ancient Greece by oligarchs,[116] it was predicated on a different rationale: ownership of property does not give some citizens a greater interest in the country than others, but it demands of some citizens greater services to the state than of others. Since the higher officers of state received no pay for their services, propertied persons were believed to be in a better position to serve the community, because their private fortunes gave them sufficient economic security to give their attention full-time to the state.[117] The idea of government by "those endowed with the personal resources" – the εὔποροι – underlies all constitutions,[118] especially oligarchies,[119] but is a prerequisite for active citizenship also in other constitutions, even democracies: the difference is merely in the amount owned.[120]

What constitutes this property? How was it valued? And who valued it? Although we have no texts that provide unequivocal answers to these questions, an attempt to raise the questions and find answers to them promises to give us some insight into aspects of the economy of the Greek states that affected their political organization. Greek has three different terms for what we translate as "property:" κτῆμα, κτῆσις, and οὐσία.[121] The first of these, κτῆμα, is most simply explained, because it always has the exclusive meaning of a "particular article of property," especially one that is intended for use (πρακτικόν): a shuttle will make a dress, other instruments will make a bed, etc.; but a κτῆμα can also be used commercially as a means of exchange: a shoe can either be worn or sold.[122] Moreover,

---

[116] Arist., *Pol.* V. 12, 1316b1–3: οἱ πολὺ ὑπερέχοντες ταῖς οὐσίαις οὐ δίκαιον οἴονται εἶναι ἴσον μετέχειν τῆς πόλεως τοὺς κεκτημένους μηθὲν τοῖς κεκτημένοις. See also VI. 3, 1318a20–21: οἱ δ' ὀλιγαρχικοὶ (*sc.* φασὶ τοῦτο δίκαιον) ὅ τι ἂν δόξῃ τῇ πλείονι οὐσίᾳ· κατὰ πλῆθος γὰρ οὐσίας φασὶ κρίνεσθαι δεῖν.

[117] I have dealt with this aspect of citizenship in Athens in Ostwald (1995a)

[118] Arist., *Pol.* VII. 9, 1329a18–21: ἀλλὰ μὴν καὶ τὰς κτήσεις δεῖ εἶναι περὶ τούτους (*sc.* those capable of bearing arms). ἀναγκαῖον γὰρ εὐπορίαν ὑπάρχειν τοῖς πολίταις, πολῖται δὲ οὗτοι. τὸ γὰρ βάναυσον οὐ μετέχει τῆς πόλεως, οὐδ' ἄλλο οὐθὲν γένος ὃ μὴ τῆς ἀρετῆς δημιουργόν ἐστιν; cf. also ibid. 5, 1326b30–6, where it is clear that the question περὶ κτήσεως καὶ τῆς περὶ τὴν οὐσίαν εὐπορίας is germane to ζῆν σχολάζοντας ἐλευθερίως ἅμα καὶ σωφρόνως. Cf. also II. 11, 1273a24–5; III. 12, 1283a18–19. Relevant is also II. 9, 1270b9–10, where the criticism of the Spartans as admitting as ephors poor men (πένητες) οἳ διὰ τὴν ἀπορίαν ὤνιοι ἦσαν, shows why poor men should not be eligible for office.

[119] See, e.g., Arist., *Pol.* III. 7, 1279b7–10; V. 4, 1303b34–7; *et passim.*

[120] See, e.g., ibid. III. 8, 1279b39–1280b6.

[121] My examination of the use of these terms will be confined to Aristotle's *Politics*, not only to keep it within reasonable bounds, but because Aristotle is more conscious of the need for a technical vocabulary than were any of his predecessors or contemporaries.

[122] Arist., *Pol.* I. 4, 1254a2–5; 9, 1257a6–16.

the use to which it is put can have a moral dimension in that it reflects on the generosity (or its lack) with which a person disposes of his property.[123]

That Aristotle counts a slave as an article of property is not surprising;[124] but it is remarkable that master and slave together are called "property" in the sense of κτῆσις.[125] A possible explanation is that κτῆσις envisages useful "property" as involving an owner along with an article owned. Considered by himself, a slave is a κτῆμα, a piece of property, who requires a master as owner to give property its functional social dimension. Although this cannot be proved, it is suggested by other uses of the term. In its most basic sense, κτῆσις, derived like κτῆμα from the verb κτάομαι ("acquire"), denotes the acquisition of property, and requires knowledge of the thing to be acquired as well as of the use to which it can be put. This knowledge can only reside in an owner. The κτῆσις of livestock, for example, involves expert knowledge of the profitability, terrain, and treatment of particular breeds (κτήματα) of horses, cattle, and sheep;[126] but it is important to note that the acquisition (κτῆσις) of inanimate property, including wealth, ranks in importance below man and his well-being:[127] possessions are seen in terms of the person(s) they are to serve. This easily glides over into a collective sense of κτῆσις: the sum total of the κτήματα a person needs for his living.[128] Natural κτῆσις, which makes us self-sufficient and has a natural limit, is acquired through pasture, piracy, agriculture, and hunting;[129] when it consists in coin (=cash), it is unnatural, since the object is used for purposes for which it was not intended by nature.[130]

Several passages discuss κτῆσις in terms of the owner rather than the property owned. The question is raised whether κτήσεις should be held in common, as proposed, for example, in Plato's *Republic*,[131] or be private; elsewhere the size, equalization, or divisibility of property are at issue.[132]

---

[123] Ibid. II. 5, 1263b11–14.

[124] Ibid. I. 4, 1253b32; 1254a10–17. Might we see here an incipient awareness that the availability of services is part of a person's assets?

[125] Ibid. III. 4, 1277a8. I see no reason for following Bernays in bracketing κτῆσις.

[126] Ibid. I. 11, 1258b13–16, cf. II. 7, 1267b10–12.

[127] Ibid. I. 13, 1259b19–21; cf. VII. 8, 1328a33–35, where it is said that the city needs κτῆσις, but that κτῆσις is not part of the city.

[128] Ibid. I. 4, 1253b23–4: ἐπεὶ οὖν ἡ κτῆσις μέρος τῆς οἰκίας ἐστὶ καὶ ἡ κτητικὴ μέρος τῆς οἰκονομίας (ἄνευ γὰρ τῶν ἀναγκαίων ἀδύνατον καὶ ζῆν καὶ εὖ ζῆν)...; 31–2: καὶ ἡ κτῆσις πλῆθος ὀργάνων ἐστί; cf. I. 8, 1256a16–17; 9, 1258a2–6; III. 9, 1280a25–27.

[129] Ibid. I. 8, 1256b4–8, 31–2.

[130] Ibid. I. 10, 1258b2–4.

[131] Ibid. II. 1, 1261a6–8; cf. also the common meals in Sparta and Crete, II. 5, 1263b39–64a16; b1–3; and VII. 10, 1329b41–1330a2.

[132] Ibid. II. 6, 1265a28–39 (cf. VII. 5, 1326b34); I.7, 1266a37–40. See the criticism

Of special interest for us are two passages in which κτῆσις is treated as the basis of the valuation, the τίμημα, through which the participation of a person in the political process is determined.[133]

This brings us to the final and most important aspect of "property", οὐσία. Etymologically, the term differs from κτῆμα and κτῆσις in that it is not rooted in the stem "acquire", "possess", but is derived from the verb "to be", suggesting that, like English "substance", it denotes the basic, core property which determines a person's status, that is, the role he plays socially and politically in his community.[134] This suggestion is borne out by an examination of all the passages in which it occurs in the *Politics*.

In a number of passages, there appears to be no difference whatever between οὐσία and κτῆσις: when, for example, Sparta is criticized for countenancing disparity in κτῆσις, which results in the ownership of far too much property (πολλὴν λίαν οὐσίαν) by some people, while others own only little (II. 9, 1270a15–18),[135] and again, when a general discussion promised – but not delivered – deals with ownership and being well-to-do in terms of property, it is hard to detect a significant difference between κτῆσις and οὐσία.[136] The same seems to be the case when, after being told that some thinkers regard regulation περὶ τὰς οὐσίας as important for inhibiting στάσις, we are given the example of Phaleas of Chalcedon, who believed that the κτήσεις of the citizens should be equal (II. 7, 1266a37–40). However, a subtle nuance may be detected in the fact that οὐσία is a single entity, while κτῆσις describes the aggregate of articles of property: if we assume the property at issue to be land, we might explain οὐσία as "estate (as a whole)" and κτῆσις as "plot of land," conceived as a constituent part of the "estate" as a whole. Other passages corroborate that οὐσία is the more substantial of the two terms and describes "property" as the steady source of one's livelihood. Small expenditures, when frequently occurring,

---

of Phaleas, esp. at II. 7, 1267b9–10. The best government allows a moderate size, VII. 11, 1295b3–5; in a democracy even the ἄποροι are to be given a small plot of land, VI .5, 1320a36–39, and both young and old receive sufficient property to discharge their civic functions, VII. 9, 1329a18, 25.

[133] Ibid. V. 6, 1306b3–16; VI. 4, 1319a17–19.

[134] There are some interesting observations on the development and philosophical use of οὐσία in Kahn (1973) 457–62, who claims that "there is no direct connection between this idiomatic <sc. non-philosophical> use of οὐσία (reflecting the possessive construction of εἰμί with the dative) and the more technical senses of οὐσία which we find in Plato and Aristotle." I am inclined to doubt this, and rather believe that the two uses are as closely linked as the two uses of "property" (of a person or of, e.g., a metal) or of "real" ("real estate" and "reality") are in English.

[135] Cf. also V. 7, 1307a35–36: ἐν Λακεδαίμονι εἰς ὀλίγους αἱ οὐσίαι ἔρχονται. – All parenthetical references in this section are to Aristotle's *Politics*.

[136] VII. 5, 1326b33–36: ὅλως περὶ κτήσεως καὶ τῆς περὶ τὴν οὐσίαν εὐπορίας.

are said to destroy estates (V. 8, 1307b33–34), and loss of οὐσία can turn political leaders into revolutionaries and tyrants (V. 12, 1316b18–25). A similar phenomenon appears at the other end of the scale in extreme democracies, when popular leaders launch malicious prosecutions against property owners (V. 5, 1304b20–24) to break up the οὐσίαι of the upper classes and confiscate their goods (κτήματα) (1305a3–7). Dionysius, tyrant of Syracuse, went so far as to tax away the entire property (οὐσία) of his subjects (V. 11, 1313b25–28). A legitimate king, on the other hand, sees to it that property owners (οἱ κεκτημένοι τὰς οὐσίας) are not treated unjustly, and that no violence is done to the common people (V. 10, 1310b40–11a2).

In criticizing the idea that common ownership of οὐσία would inhibit litigation, Aristotle argues that conflict is much more likely to arise among people who own οὐσίαι in common than among those who own their κτήσεις individually (II. 5, 1263b15–27). Again, in his discussion of Plato's "communism" Aristotle brackets common ownership of οὐσία with that of wives and children (II. 3, 1261b20–27); but he also criticizes Plato for regulating οὐσία by equalizing the κτήσεις of the citizens without considering control of procreation (τεκνοποιία).[137] Here, too, οὐσία seems to connote the "estate," κτήσεις its constituent parts. Much the same distinctions are found in Aristotle's discussion of the ideas of Phaleas of Chalcedon, to which we have already alluded. Phaleas believed that crime is caused by the "inequality in κτήσεις" and therefore proposed the enactment of "equality of property" (ἰσότης τῆς οὐσίας) to inhibit it; a modicum of οὐσία combined with cultivation (ἐργασία) will, he thought, supply a person with the necessities of life (II. 7, 1266b40–67a10; cf. 1266b25–33). At the same time, however, Aristotle criticizes Phaleas for treating οὐσία exclusively in terms of ownership of land (τὴν τῆς γῆς κτῆσιν), and for excluding considerations of wealth in slaves, cattle, coin, and equipment from his proposed equalization (II. 7, 1267b9–13).[138] This permits the inference that while ownership of land was the primary connotation of οὐσία, it was not confined to it, but also included (or could include) other assets that were seen as determining the quality of life.

This is corroborated in several ways. Aristotle criticizes, for example, the uneven distribution of property (ἀνωμαλία τῆς κτήσεως) in Sparta, by stating that some people's estates have come to be so large (πολλὴν λίαν οὐσίαν) that the land has fallen into the hands of the few (II. 9, 1270a15–18; cf. V. 7, 1307a35–36). He recommends that inheritance laws in a

---

[137] II. 6, 1265a31–b11, esp. b6–7: μᾶλλον δὲ δεῖν ὑπολάβοι τις ἂν ὡρίσθαι τῆς οὐσίας τὴν τεκνοποιίαν. Cf. also 7, 1266b8–13.

[138] At II. 12, 1274b9–11, there is a neat summary: Φαλέου δ' ἴδιον ἡ τῶν οὐσιῶν ἀνομάλωσις, Πλάτωνος δ' ἥ τε τῶν γυναικῶν καὶ παίδων καὶ τῆς οὐσίας κοινότης.

democracy aim at levelling the extent of οὐσίαι, so that the more indigent (ἄποροι) advance to a status of εὔποροι (V. 8, 1309a25–26),[139] but he also sees a danger in that equalization of property may upset the balance beween the well-to-do and the masses and result in the emergence of a different kind of régime (V. 9, 1309b39–10a2). He rebukes Plato for inconsistently excluding ownership of land when stipulating in the *Laws* that the total size of an estate (τὴν πᾶσαν οὐσίαν), i.e. the sum of all its assets, must not exceed five times the size of the smallest (II. 6, 1265b21–23). Also he seems to think primarily of agriculture when he speaks of the use of slaves in Book VII (10, 1330a30–31): public slaves ought to be used for the cultivation of public land, while owners of private property (ἰδίους τῶν κεκτημένων τὰς οὐσίας) should use privately-owned slaves. Most telling is the fact that he classifies an estate consisting exclusively of monetary assets (τὴν τοῦ νομίσματος οὐσίαν) among the κτήσεις that are not conducive to the good life: the use of monetary assets has no limits, because it consists in the pointless accumulation of capital (I. 9, 1257b35–58a1); a sharp contrast between monetary and landed οὐσία is implied.

This leads to the question of the amount of οὐσία required for the good life, especially of the community. More usually than not Aristotle uses οὐσία rather κτῆσις in describing the estate whose size determines the social and political status of a person plays in the state.

Only one passage attributes to οὐσία a role in external affairs: the amount of land (πλῆθος οὐσίας) owned by a given community should not be so large as to tempt a stronger neighbor to annex it (II.7, 1267a28–37). Theoretical discussions advocate that the size of estates be proportionate to the size of the population of the state,[140] and emphasize that an equal distribution of landed property (ἡ τῆς οὐσίας ὁμαλότης) has an impact on the social and political structure of the community. To make sure that every citizen has a modicum of landed property, some states put restrictions on the sale of land (οὐσία) (II. 7, 1266b14–33).

---

[139] In the context of inheritance belongs also the story told about the two brothers from Histiaea, related at V. 4, 1303b34–7: the δημοτικοί supported the demands of the less well-to-do brother (ἀπορώτερος), to compel his rich sibling (οὐσίαν πολλὴν ἔχων), who was supported by the εὔποροι, to show him the οὐσία and the treasure bequeathed by their father.

[140] II. 7, 1266b8–13.

C. PROPERTY VALUATION

The Greeks thought of citizenship as "having a share in the state," μετέχειν τῆς πολιτείας.[141] Possession (or lack) of property (οὐσία) played in all ancient Greek states a part in defining the size of the share prerequisite for citizenship. Now that we have seen that the property by which the degree of participation in the community was determined primarily in terms of ownership of land, we must examine the mechanism by which the amount of land owned was translated into the degree of participation by each citizen in public affairs. The minimum share allowed participation in the Assembly, the public meetings of the community; the maximum made a citizen eligible to high office. For political purposes the size of a person's property was fixed by a property valuation called τίμημα,[142] and on its basis his share in the community was established. Although its size determined participation in public affairs most decisively in oligarchies,[143] our most detailed knowledge derives from the role it played in democratizing Athens.

Property valuation (τίμημα) is said to have existed in Attica even before Solon as the basis for dividing the citizen population into four property classes (τέλη).[144] When it started and how it was conducted is veiled in the mists of history. Probability favors some time in the eighth and seventh centuries B.C.E. for its institution, when the public burdens so far borne by aristocrats devolved on society as a whole, especially the upper classes.[145] Although it played some part in democracies,[146] it was always a hallmark of oligarchies.[147] By the fourth century, the instution of valuation was laid

---

[141] I have discussed this problem in Ostwald (1996) 49–61. Cf. also Walter (1993) 23–27

[142] That the τίμημα was based on ownership of property is attested by: Pl., *Resp.* VIII. 551b, *Lg.* V. 744a–d, X. 915b; Dem. XXVII (*Aphobus 1*) 7, XXIX (*Aphobus 3*) 60; Arist., *Pol.* II. 7, 1266b25; IV.5, 1292a41, 6, 1292b30–32; 14, 1298a38–40; V.6, 1306b12–13; VI.6, 1320b25–26; 7, 1321a28. The following discussion will exclude from consideration the judicial sense of τίμημα, the fine or penalty proposed upon conviction by plaintiff and counterproposed by defendant. For this meaning, see Busolt-Swoboda (1920) I. 553–54. The best (though partly antiquated) discussion is still that of Böckh (1886) I. 578–94.

[143] Pl., *Resp.* VIII. 550cd, 551b, 553a; Arist., *Rhet.* I. 8, 1365b33; *Pol.* IV. 5, 1292a39–40; 6, 1292b31–32; V. 7, 1307a27–28.

[144] Arist., *Ath.Pol.* 7. 3; cf. Hsch., *s.vv.* ἐκ τιμημάτων, ζευγίσιον, θητικόν, ἱππάδα; and *Suda, s.v.* ἐκ τιμημάτων.

[145] I have touched on this problem in Ostwald (1995a) 373–75.

[146] E.g., Arist., *Pol.* IV. 4, 1291b39–40; 9, 1294b3–4; VI.2, 1317b22–23.

[147] Ibid. II. 6, 1266a12–14; III. 5, 1278a21–23; IV. 5, 1292a39–b4; 9, 1294b4 and 10; *Rhet.* I. 8, 1365b33.

down by law, at least in some states;[148] the valuating (τίμησις) was probably done by the property owners themselves every few years,[149] and was subsequently entered into a public register.[150] The concrete evidence for such registers is very meagre indeed. But we know that in Athens the ληξιαρχικὸν γραμματεῖον, a public register kept by each deme, recorded in the fourth century not only the names of the members of each deme but also the land each owned.[151] The lists of citizens, which are attested in many other states, including oligarchies, will certainly have included entries on the property of each individual,[152] since ownership of property served, among other things, as the basis for the assignment of military obligations.[153]

In Athens the τιμήματα allowed Solon to group the citizenry into four τέλη to determine the liability of each citizen to service to the community,[154] presumably because, in the absence of a paid civil service, those of sufficient means not to have to work for a living were expected to give their time and energy to the state. Just as in Athens only members of the highest τέλος, the *pentakosiomedimnoi*, were called upon to serve as archons or treasurers,[155] high property valuations were *a fortiori* a prerequisite for high office in oligarchies.[156] Some oligarchies required moderate valuations even for the franchise.[157] Democracies usually admitted any free-born

---

[148] See Arist., *Pol.* IV. 6, 1292b30.

[149] This is suggested by the use of the middle voice in Lys. XIX (*Aristophanes*) 48, and in Is. VII (*Apollodorus*) 39. According to Arist., *Pol.* V. 8, 1308a35–b4, it was made annually in some states and every three or five years in larger states.

[150] Lys. XVII (*Eraton*) 7–9. For the existence and range of public registers in general, see Weiss (1923) 369–87.

[151] See Ostwald (1995a) 377–78. Cf. Sickinger (1999) 51–60.

[152] I know of no systematic study of such lists outside Athens. The use of γράφεσθαι and its compounds both in Athens and outside in decrees granting citizenship indicates the existence of registers kept by some civic unit or other; see Osborne (1983) 158 and 171–81, and more recently, Jones (1991) 79–102.

[153] See Beloch (1906) 42–51, cf. Busolt-Swoboda (1920) I. 564, n. 2; 577, n. 2.

[154] Arist., *Ath.Pol.* 7. 3–4; Is. VII (*Apollodorus*) 39; Dem. XXIV (*Timocrates*) 144, XLIII (*Macartatus*) 54. Plato, *Lg.* III. 698b; Harp., *s.v.* ἱππάς; Hsch., *s.v.* ὁμοτελεῖς. For this formulation, see my article cited above, n. 117. Note that Plato's state in the *Laws* also recognizes four τέλη (V. 744a–d, cf. Arist., *Pol.* II, 6, 1266a16–17).

[155] Arist., *Ath.Pol.* 7. 3 with 8. 1.

[156] Xen., *Mem.* IV. 6.12; Arist., *Rhet.* I. 8, 1365b33; *Pol.* II. 7, 1266b23–24; III. 5, 1278a23; 11, 1282a31–32; IV. 4, 1291b39–40; 5, 1292a39–40, b1; IV. 9, 1294b9–10; V. 5, 1305a29–30; VI. 2, 1317b22; 4, 1318b30–31.

[157] Arist., *Pol.* II. 6, 1266a8–13; 7, 1266b23–24; III. 5, 1278a21–26; 11, 1282a29–31; IV. 5, 1292b1–3; 9, 1294b3–4; V. 5, 1305a30–31; 6, 1305b32–33; VI. 3, 1318a30–38.

male adult, propertied or not, to citizenship;[158] in Solonian Athens the lowest political class, the *thetes,* counted as a τέλος and were thus able to exercise the franchise and man the people's courts, even though they had no property to valuate.[159] The recognition of the unpropertied *thetes* as a τέλος is probably Solon's single most crucial contribution to the later development of democracy.

The term τέλη was used to describe both the contributions to the community expected from its members in proportion to their τιμήματα, and the property groups that made these contributions. Contributions took the form of service as public officials as well as military service,[160] the performance of expensive liturgies,[161] and providing a dowry for female relatives whose deceased fathers had been *thetes* i.e., had died without leaving them a dowry.[162] If we call these contributions "taxes" we must remember that they were neither levied on all citizens alike nor "payable" at regular intervals, but performances of public functions demanded by situations as they arose.

D. "WELL-TO-DO" AND "INDIGENT" IN OLIGARCHY AND DEMOCRACY

Aristotle characterizes citizenship as "participation" in the socio-political community (μετέχειν τῆς πολιτείας), implying that it is not viewed as a *right* a person possesses, which may or may not be exercised, but as a share essential to the functioning of a larger entity.[163] This does not mean that "rights" are not implied in the notion of "participation," but they are

---

[158] Ibid. III. 11, 1282a29; IV. 9, 1294b3–4; V. 5, 1305a29–30; VI. 2, 1317b22–23.

[159] Arist., *Ath.Pol.* 7. 3–4; Harpocr., *s.vv.* θῆτες καὶ θητικόν, and ἱππάς, Suda, *s.v.* ἱππάς, Pollux VIII. 130–31.

[160] Thuc. VI. 43; Antiphon, fr. 61 (Blass-Thalheim); Harpocr., *s.v.* θῆτες καὶ θητικόν, with Rhodes (1981) 138, 142–3.

[161] Xen, *Oec.* II. 6, mentions raising horses for the cavalry (ἱπποτροφία), paying for equipping and training choruses for the dramatic festivals (χορηγία), training and equipping runners for public festivals (γυμνασισαρχία), sponsoring civic and religious affairs (προστατεῖα), equipping and maintaining triremes (τριηραρχία), and payment of special property taxes (εἰσφορά); see Pomeroy (1994) 225–28. Antiphon V (*Herodes*) 77 shows that τέλη involve civic contributions to one's own city, while λητουργίαι could be undertaken either for one's own or a foreign city.

[162] Law in Dem. XLIII (*Macartatus*) 54; Harpocr., *s.v.* θῆτες καὶ θητικόν. – For another social function of the τέλη, an injunction barring the arrest of any person who can provide three sureties from his own τέλος class, see the bouleutic oath in Dem. XXIV (*Timocrates*) 144.

[163] See the discussions cited in n. 141 above.

"rights" only in our sense of the term: the Greek language lacks the concept. On this criterion Aristotle explicitly excludes certain groups from the definition of "citizen": (a) naturalized persons (because they were excluded from holding archonships and priesthoods at Athens, and presumably elsewhere), (b) residents (such as metics and slaves), who, by having access to a court of law, enjoy a right that can be extended by treaty also to aliens: and (c) the very young and the very old, because they can not yet or can no longer function as active citizens (*Pol.* III.1, 1275a5–19). The exclusion of women is taken for granted and left unmentioned, because women were not regarded as full legal and political persons in any part of the Greek – or, for that matter, ancient – world,[164] and so is the exclusion of slaves, because they functioned as no more than "animate tools," and not as persons in their own right: they were the property, i.e. extension, of their free masters.

Still, even an adult male not encumbered with any of these disabilities – that is, a native of his city, born of at least one citizen parent and enjoying the rights to elect public officials, to be himself eligible for public office, and to cast his vote in making political or judicial decisions[165] – may, in the eyes of Aristotle as well as for most Greek states of his time, have fulfilled only necessary but not sufficient conditions for full citizenship. For in the best state, Aristotle tells us, a βάναυσος τεχνίτης, an industrial worker, defined as a person who lives off the work of his own hands (1277a37–b1), will not be a citizen, because the exercise of citizenship is possible only for those "who have no need to work for a living."[166] In other words, to be a citizen a person must be equipped with the necessities of life in order to have the leisure required for functioning as a citizen (II. 11, 1273a35–6; cf. 1273b6–7); the term used for a person so equipped is εὔπορος, his condition is εὐπορία, also expressed by the verb εὐπορεῖν;[167] absence of or

---

[164] A possible exception are the Issedonians, see Hdt. IV. 26.2.

[165] Ar. *Pol.* III. 1, 1275a22–3: πολίτης δ' ἁπλῶς οὐδενὶ τῶν ἄλλων ὁρίζεται μᾶλλον ἢ τῷ μετέχειν κρίσεως καὶ ἀρχῆς.

[166] Ibid. 5, 1278a8–11: ἡ δὲ βελτίστη πόλις οὐ ποιήσει βάναυσον πολίτην. εἰ δὲ καὶ οὗτος πολίτης, ἀλλὰ πολίτου ἀρετὴν ἣν εἴπομεν λεκτέον οὐ παντός, οὐδ' ἐλευθέρου μόνον, ἀλλ' ὅσοι τῶν ἔργων εἰσὶν ἀφειμένοι τῶν ἀναγκαίων. That Aristotle is not alone, nor the first one, to hold this belief is shown by the argument of the Herald at Eur., *Suppl.* 421–25, that a farmer is prevented by his work from devoting himself to public affairs.

[167] Ibid. VII. 9, 1329a18–21: ἀλλὰ μὴν καὶ τὰς κτήσεις δεῖ εἶναι περὶ τούτους. ἀναγκαῖον γὰρ εὐπορίαν ὑπάρχειν τοῖς πολίταις, πολῖται δὲ οὗτοι. τὸ γὰρ βάναυσον οὐ μετέχει τῆς πόλεως, οὐδ' ἄλλο οὐθὲν γένος ὃ μὴ τῆς ἀρετῆς δημιουργόν ἐστιν; cf. also ibid. 5, 1326b30–6, where it is clear that the question περὶ κτήσεως καὶ τῆς περὶ τὴν οὐσίαν εὐπορίας is germane to ζῆν σχολάζοντας ἐλευθερίως ἅμα καὶ σωφρόνως.

deficiency in meeting these minimal requirements is expressed by ἄπορος, ἀπορία, and ἀπορεῖν.[168]

Although Aristotle confines exclusion of industrial workers to the "best state" (βελτίστη πόλις) and thus admits them to an oligarchy or a democracy, his argument helps us understand the role of property in these two "perverted" constitutional forms. It goes without saying that a wealthy man, a πλούσιος, will automatically be εὔπορος ("well-to-do") and that a poor man, a πένης, will automatically be ἄπορος ("indigent"): many passages in the *Politics* suggest that Aristotle did indeed see a close relation between these two pairs.[169] However, he never treats them as synonymous and provides no justification to those modern translators who treat them as identical in meaning. Since "wealth" and "poverty" are economic terms, it is tempting to assume that πλούσιος and πένης express the economic status of an individual or society, and to look for a suitable meaning for εὔπορος and ἄπορος in the social or political sphere. Such a proceeding is not, as we shall see, conducive to reliable results, not only because social, economic, and political spheres, differentiated in our own conceptual framework, were not clearly separated from one another by the Greeks, but also because these three aspects are in most instances so closely intertwined in Aristotle that we shall have to be on our guard lest an attempt to disentangle them create confusion rather than clarification. It will, therefore, be more fruitful to define the εὐπορ- and ἀπορ-stems in terms of the areas to which Aristotle applies them.

Like πλούσιος and πένης, εὔπορος, ἄπορος and their cognates carry predominantly material connotations. But, unlike πλούσιος and πένης, these connotations always envisage a specific function for the performance of which material possessions are needed, without which it cannot be performed. When followed by a genitive, they predicate the possession (or lack) of whatever qualifies a person or corporate entity to perform a given function. In private life, for example, a man rich in coined money might not possess the kind of wealth that will keep him from starving (I. 9, 1257b14–15: τοιοῦτον...πλοῦτον οὗ εὐπορῶν λιμῷ ἀπολεῖται); again, although the exclusive pursuit of philosophy had reduced Thales to poverty (πενία), he still disposed of a small sum of money (εὐπορήσαντα χρημάτων ὀλίγων) to make a downpayment on all the olive-presses in Miletus and Chios, whose possession enabled him to establish a monopoly to confound his

---

[168] II. 11, 1273a24–5; III. 12, 1283a18–19. Relevant is also II. 9, 1270b9–10, where the criticism of the Spartans as admitting as ephors poor men (πένητες) οἳ διὰ τὴν ἀπορίαν ὤνιοι ἦσαν, shows why poor men should not be eligible for office.

[169] See, e.g., IV. 4, 1291b2–8. For some astute observations on this point, see White (1992) 194–95.

d. "Well-to-do" and "indigent" in oligarchy and democracy 55

detractors (I. 11, 1259a6–19). In other words, while πένεσθαι and πλουτεῖν are mutually exclusive (IV. 4, 1291b7–8), there are occasions when a poor man (πένης) can be well-to-do (εὔπορος), and, we may surmise, a rich man ἄπορος. Negatively, the agrarian reforms advocated by Hippodamus of Miletus are criticized for not being viable if they entail that the same person must farm public land in addition to his own: the amount he will be able to harvest will be insufficient (II. 8, 1268a41–b1: ἄπορον ἔσται τῶν καρπῶν) to maintain both a military household and his own. Elsewhere, the community is urged to see to it that none of its citizens lack food (ἀπορεῖν τροφῆς), and common meals are to be instituted to this end at public expense, so that the indigent (ἀποροῦντες) will not have to make contributions to the community out of their own meagre resources (VII. 10, 1330a1–8).[170]

In public life, εὐπορία and ἀπορία may describe the requirements of a state. Proximity to the sea, for instance, is desirable for a steady supply of the necessities of life (VII. 6, 1327a18–20: πρὸς εὐπορίαν τῶν ἀναγκαίων), and financial solvency (VII. 8, 1328b10–11: χρημάτων τινὰ εὐπορίαν)[171] is required for meeting domestic and military needs. Moreover, a generous supply of revenues (προσόδων εὐπορία) makes possible the widest degree of participation of the citizens in the fourth type of democracy in that it provides the means to supplement the marginal assets of the ἄποροι, so as to give them sufficient leisure to participate in public affairs. This may give the indigent an advantage over the wealthy: being now in a position regularly to attend the meetings of the Assembly and the jury courts, they will exercise an authority exceeding that of the laws, whereas the πλούσιοι will often be prevented by having to pay attention to their private affairs from making themselves heard at such meetings (IV. 6, 1292b41–1293a11). In short, the προσόδων εὐπορία here reverses the norm: the indigent will get the leisure needed to run the state, whereas those whose wealth normally frees them for public service have to attend to their private affairs to an extent that inhibits their participation in political and judicial matters. Further, the availability of funds to pay for public service (εὐπορία μισθοῦ) in this kind of democracy will tend to erode the power of a Council, because its functions are made redundant by frequent Assembly meetings (IV. 15, 1299b38–1300a4); where no such funds are available, the Council is the most populist institution (VI. 2, 1317b30–5). An increase in the supply of ready cash (εὐπορία νομίσματος) may lead to revolutionary change in oligarchies and polities, unless it is accompanied by a change in the assessment system (V. 8, 1308a35–8). Finally, a εὐπορία of an entirely different kind may determine admission to citizenship: when a population

---

[170] This is evidently intended to avoid the Spartan practice, see II. 9, 1271a29–37.
[171] For the opposite, see I. 11, 1259a22: ὅταν ἀπορῶσι χρημάτων.

falls short of a desirable number of legitimate citizens (ἔνδεια τῶν γνησίων πολιτῶν), many states admit to citizenship persons of foreign or illegitimate birth, including those whose claim to citizenship rests on the citizenship of their mother alone; when there is no manpower shortage, however (εὐποροῦντες δὴ ὄχλου), persons are progressively disqualified, until only those of two citizen parents are entitled to citizenship (III. 5, 1278a29–34).

In short, the εὐπορ- and ἄπορ-stems, usually when followed by a genitive, indicate the presence or absence of factors required for performing a given function. In most cases the genitive refers to such material resources as money, revenues, coinage, and pay, but it may also describe the necessities of life, an adequate harvest, or a viable size of population. In no case does the possession of these requirements make a man or state automatically wealthy (πλούσιος) or their lack poor (πένης).

We next turn to the use of these terms in Aristotle's analysis of social and political institutions. Aristotle emphasizes the composite nature of the state in the very first chapter of *Politics* I (1252a18–23) and on several occasions thereafter.[172] εὐπορ-qualities figure prominently in three different lists of constituent parts of the state.[173] In a list designed to show how the divisions of society explain the variety of constitutional forms, a distinction between εὔποροι, ἄποροι, and μέσοι[174] is introduced immediately after "families" (οἰκίαι) to pave the way for differentiating upper from lower classes: the εὔποροι are defined as capable of providing their own arms (τὸ ὁπλιτικόν), while the ἄποροι are not able to do so (τὸ ἄνοπλον). In short, the three terms refer to the resources from which each class contributes to the political and military structure of the state.[175] In classifying the prerequisites for the proper functioning of the state, on the other hand, the εὔποροι are listed as seventh in importance[176] after farmers, industrial workers, merchants, unskilled laborers, and the military as "the class that supports civic activities with its estates" (IV. 4, 1291a33–4: τὸ ταῖς οὐσίαις λειτουργοῦν). Here there are neither ἄποροι with whom they are contrasted, nor are they termed πλούσιοι, even though there can be

---

[172] I. 1, 1252a18–23; III. 3, 1276b6–9; IV. 3, 1289b27–8; 4, 1290b23–4, 38–9; VII. 8, 1328a21–7.

[173] The lack of consistency among the lists at IV. 3, IV. 4, and VII. 8 has unnecessarily disturbed some modern scholars, who do not recognize that the character of each list is determined by its context. Despite inevitable overlaps, none of the three claims to be definitive.

[174] For the same three classes, see IV. 11, 1295b1–3.

[175] IV. 3, 1289b27–1290a5. Barker's translation (1948) 160 as "the rich, the poor, and the middle class" makes little sense in the context. Cf. VI. 7, 1321a12–13.

[176] Or sixth, since the sixth slot is unfilled; cf. Barker (1948) 166 n. 1.

little doubt that they were, in fact, wealthy. What seems to matter in the present context is that they possess the wherewithal to support public activities: activities that keep the community alive enjoy a higher priority than the economic basis on which it rests.

This is corroborated by the final item on Aristotle's list, which is similar in purpose and ranking, except that it forms part of Aristotle's account of the ideal state and claims to be oriented toward different professional groups (κατὰ τὰς ἐργασίας): merchants and unskilled laborers are omitted, while a priestly class and a decision-making class (κριτὰς τῶν ἀναγκαίων καὶ συμφερόντων) are added after τὸ εὔπορον, which is defined as "making available a supply of money for the state's internal and military needs."[177] It is likely that Aristotle regarded this class as identical with the propertied class which provides liturgies at IV. 4, 1291a33–4.

Accordingly, the two groups, well-to-do and indigent, are, for Aristotle, essential for the functioning of any socio-political community. While the same person may have the capacity of discharging different functions – a soldier can also be a farmer or an artisan – the same person cannot in fact be both rich and poor, that is, both have and not have the material resources to undertake public service. Therefore, the well-to-do and the indigent are parts of the state in a special sense.[178] It is worth observing that the relation here noted between πλουτεῖν-εὔποροι and πένεσθαι-ἄποροι does not imply that only a rich man can be εὔπορος or that all ἄποροι are poor; the point is merely that wealth provides the means for fulfilling all functions of an active citizen. At the same time, the existence of groups of ἄποροι and of εὔποροι is more indispensable for democracies and oligarchies than it is for aristocracies, since the number of the well-to-do always exceeds the number of the noble and well-born.[179]

We have so far concentrated on the analytical side of Aristotle's discussion of the preconditions of citizenship. A few words need to be added about some relevant prescriptive elements. Since ἄποροι and εὔποροι are

---

[177] VII. 8, 1328b5–23, esp. 11–12: ἔτι χρημάτων τινὰ εὐπορίαν, ὅπως ἔχωσι καὶ πρὸς τὰς καθ' αὑτοὺς χρείας καὶ πρὸς <τὰς> πολεμικάς.

[178] IV. 4, 1291b2–8: τὰς μὲν οὖν ἄλλας δυνάμεις τοῖς αὐτοῖς ὑπάρχειν ἐνδέχεσθαι δοκεῖ πολλοῖς, οἷον τοὺς αὐτοὺς εἶναι τοὺς προπολεμοῦντας καὶ γεωργοῦντας καὶ τεχνίτας, ἔτι δὲ τοὺς βουλευομένους τε καὶ κρίνοντας· ἀντιποιοῦνται δὲ καὶ τῆς ἀρετῆς πάντες, καὶ τὰς πλείστας ἀρχὰς ἄρχειν οἴονται δύνασθαι· ἀλλὰ πένεσθαι καὶ πλουτεῖν τοὺς αὐτοὺς ἀδύνατον. διὸ ταῦτα μέρη μάλιστα εἶναι δοκεῖ πόλεως, οἱ εὔποροι καὶ οἱ ἄποροι. For Thales as an exception, see I. 11, 1259a6–19, as discussed above, pp. 54–55.

[179] V. 1, 1301b39–1302a2: διὸ καὶ μάλιστα δύο γίνονται πολιτεῖαι, δῆμος καὶ ὀλιγαρχία· εὐγένεια γὰρ καὶ ἀρετὴ ἐν ὀλίγοις, ταῦτα δ' ἐν πλείοσιν· εὐγενεῖς γὰρ καὶ ἀγαθοὶ οὐδαμοῦ ἑκατόν, εὔποροι δὲ πολλοὶ πανταχοῦ.

vital constitutive factors of both democracies and oligarchies, their existence may pose a threat to a régime, if a balance between the two groups is not carefully maintained. Stability is most effectively achieved by vesting power in a middle class; yet this is hard to do in small democratic states, which frequently have only the two classes, well-to-do and indigent, and therefore run the risk of destruction if the indigent should prevail numerically (IV. 11, 1296a7–18). Every effort must, therefore, be made to encourage each group to let the other take a hand in running the magistracies and in participating in political action, either by mixing well-to-do and indigent or by fostering the middle class (V. 8, 1308b25–31) without, however, jeopardizing the identity of either group. Since the existence of both is vital for the survival of democracies as well as of oligarchies, the introduction of equality of property into either régime will inevitably make for a different constitutional form. It is, therefore, wrong for demagogues to inveigh against the well-to-do: they ought rather to rise to their defence (V. 9, 1309b38–1310a6). The maintenance of the identity of each group is essential even for the preservation of tyranny: a tyrant should inculcate in both the well-to-do and the indigent the belief that their preservation depends on him, he should prevent the two groups from giving offense one to the other, and he should give the stronger of the two a stake in his rule (V. 11, 1315a31–40).

To sum up: for Aristotle a class of people sufficiently well-off to devote itself to the affairs of state is as vital a constituent part of society as is a class not so endowed; the two classes must remain in balance with one another – a political and social balance that involves an imbalance in property owned – for that society to preserve its constitutional character. The well-to-do class may, but need not be wealthy, and the less privileged class may, but need not be poor; what matters is that one class has sufficient property to afford it the leisure to engage actively in politics, and that it does not use its status to deny the indigent some degree of participation in the political process.

If, thus, a minimum of affluence is required for the active exercise of citizenship, we should expect it to be required *a fortiori* for eligibility to public office. Curiously enough, there is no explicit general statement of this principle anywhere in the *Politics*, but it appears in a number of guises in specific contexts. Aristotle approves, for example, of the Carthaginian practice of basing the appointment of king and general on both wealth and merit, on the grounds that an indigent person (ἀποροῦντα) cannot have the leisure necessary to be a good ruler (II. 11, 1273a23–5); but he also disapproves of the practice of offering high office for sale on the grounds that this puts a greater premium on wealth than on meritorious ruling, for which the leisure of the well-to-do (εὐπορία) is a precondition (ibid. 35–9).

d. "Well-to-do" and "indigent" in oligarchy and democracy

Instead, he suggests, those most capable of governing ought to be encouraged to govern: if legislation cannot provide for the εὐπορία of all decent men, it should at least provide the magistrates with the leisure they need to govern.[180]

A slightly different perspective on the role of εὐπορία and ἀπορία in the appointment of magistrates appears in the classification of constitutions in Book IV. In defining a constitution as the organization of magistracies in a given state, determined by eligibility to office in terms either of the group that dominates the citizen body or of an equality shared by the groups,[181] Aristotle envisages the possibility that in some constitutions – no doubt democracies – those who have to work for a living, the ἄποροι, are eligible for public office; their leisure can be assumed to be purchased by public pay.[182] εὔπορος comes here close to being equated with πλούσιος and ἄπορος with πένης.

Before we come to a discussion of the dominance of εὔποροι-πλούσιοι in oligarchies and of ἄποροι-πένητες in democracies, a few more passages in which these terms are associated with magistracies deserve consideration. One definition of oligarchy stresses the requirement that the well-to-do (εὔποροι), their inferior numbers notwithstanding, occupy the magistracies, whereas in a democracy the indigent (ἄποροι) hold office because they constitute the numerical majority (III. 8, 1279b28–31).[183] That the lower limit of εὐπορία need imply neither significant wealth nor oligarchy is shown by the statement that Solon excluded from eligibility to office only the *thetes*, the only electoral class for which there was no property requirement, but included the *zeugitai*, the lowest propertied class, among the eligible εὔποροι (II. 12, 1274b15–21). Finally, the well-to-do figure in the appointment to public office in "polities," that is, in those constitutions which combine the best features of oligarchy and democracy. In polities society consists of a public-spirited class (γένος πολιτικόν) "capable of

---

[180] II. 11, 1273b5–7. Following Spengel, I prefer ἄρχειν to Ross's ἀργεῖν at line 5.

[181] IV. 3, 1290a7–13. See above, pp. 41–42 with n. 111.

[182] There is no explicit statement to substantiate this assumption, but something of the sort can be inferred from IV. 9, 1294a37–42, where it is stated that oligarchies impose a fine on those εὔποροι who fail to appear for jury duty, but do not pay ἄποροι jurors, whereas democracies pay ἄποροι jurors but do not penalize εὔποροι absentees. Cf. also the contention at IV. 13, 1297b6–12, that πένητες are content to acquiesce in their ineligibility to office so long as they are not humiliated and their property is left intact, but that they refuse to go to war, unless they are paid a subsistence allowance and are relieved of some consequences of being ἄποροι.

[183] Cf. also IV. 4, 1290a30–b3, as quoted above, n. 113. Mention ought to be made here of states (*not* individuals) which are so well off that they entrust menial offices to slaves, see IV. 15, 1299a24.

being ruled and ruling in conformity with a law which assigns office to the well-to-do (εὔποροι) on the basis of merit."[184] The requirement of merit indicates that eligibility is predicated not merely on εὐπορία in terms of wealth but in terms of sufficient moral assets to vouchsafe a character as well as material assets to afford the leisure suitable for high office.[185]

Belonging to the well-to-do and being wealthy confer, in Aristotle's opinion, an elevated social status. We have already cited his view that quantitative considerations of majority and minority rule are not the decisive factors in defining democracy and oligarchy, and that the domination of a majority of εὔποροι by a minority of πένητες does not constitute an oligarchy.[186] It is significant that those here called εὔποροι are elsewhere in the same passage referred to as πλούσιοι (1290a34–5, b3); the opposite group is only referred to as πένητες, no doubt because the poor cannot be regarded as ἄποροι when they possess greater authority than the wealthy. But the fact that the wealthy are named as εὔποροι indicates that, though politically dominated, their social status remains superior to the status of those who dominate them. A similar social distinction seems implied, when the opposing sides in civil strife and conflicts (στάσεις καὶ μάχας) are called δῆμος (common people) and εὔποροι (well-to-do), respectively (IV. 11, 1296a27–32), or when in the establishment of aristocracies too much power is given to the εὔποροι at the expense of the common people on the grounds that "the greed of the wealthy (τῶν πλουσίων) is more prone to ruin the state than that of the commons."[187] Evidently, the wealthy are identical with the εὔποροι; they are likely to be given greater power in an aristocracy because of their superior social status, but it is through their economic status as πλούσιοι that they threaten the state. The higher social status that accompanies the well-to-do emerges also from their association with τιμαί (honors) and with the kind of leisure which, in archaic times, led to a more magnanimous pursuit of excellence (VII. 13, 1332a15–16; VIII. 6, 1341a28–9), made explicit in the definition of "polity": polities "which have an oligarchical bias are closer to aristocracies, since education and noble birth are more intimately linked to being well-to-do (τοῖς εὐπορωτέ-

---

[184] III. 17, 1288a13–15: ... γένος πολιτικὸν δυνάμενον ἄρχεσθαι καὶ ἄρχειν κατὰ νόμον τὸν κατ' ἀξίαν διανέμοντα τοῖς εὐπόροις τὰς ἀρχάς.

[185] Barker (1948) 151 (Note GG) gets involved in unnecessary difficulties by erroneously equating the εὔποροι with the wealthy.

[186] IV. 4, 1290a30–40, esp. 37–40, as cited above, n. 113.

[187] IV. 12, 1297a7–13: διαμαρτάνουσι δὲ πολλοὶ καὶ τῶν τὰς ἀριστοκρατικὰς βουλομένων ποιεῖν πολιτείας, οὐ μόνον ἐν τῷ πλεῖον νέμειν τοῖς εὐπόροις, ἀλλὰ καὶ ἐν τῷ παρακρούεσθαι τὸν δῆμον. ἀνάγκη γὰρ χρόνῳ ποτὲ ἐκ τῶν ψευδῶν ἀγαθῶν ἀληθὲς συμβῆναι κακόν· αἱ γὰρ πλεονεξίαι τῶν πλουσίων ἀπολλύασι μᾶλλον τὴν πολιτείαν ἢ αἱ τοῦ δήμου.

d. "Well-to-do" and "indigent" in oligarchy and democracy 61

ροις), and further, the well-to-do are regarded as having those qualities the lack of which causes crimes to be committed: that is why people call them 'gentlemen' and 'prominent'."[188] The qualities here attributed to εὐπορία clearly go beyond wealth and include also the prestige that goes with high social standing.

The advantages enjoyed by the εὔποροι over against the ἄποροι are frequently the cause of that split in civil society that the Greeks called στάσις. The affinity of the well-to-do to wealth and of the indigent to poverty is made poignant in a passage which illustrates incidentally how personal altercations among the upper class (γνώριμοι) can inflame passions that spread through the state: after the Persian Wars, two brothers quarrelled at Histiaea about the inheritance their father had left. One brother, described as "more indigent" (ἀπορώτερος) objected that his sibling "was not making public either the estate or the treasure their father had found," and rallied the populists to his side; the other brother, "who had a substantial estate" appealed to the well-to-do (εὔποροι).[189] Neither brother is likely to have been poor, since both belonged to the upper class (γνώριμοι); what made one more indigent than the other can only be guessed: most probably he was the younger, perhaps still unmarried, while his older brother had married into a rich family and had received a substantial dowry. That the latter should turn for support to the εὔποροι is only to be expected; what seems remarkable is that the more indigent brother, though far from poor, seems to have been so successful in his appeal to the populists, who, since they are not called ἄποροι, are less likely to have been the lower classes than members of the upper class whose outlook was sympathetic to the common people. Though triggered by a personal dispute about property, the resulting conflict seems to have been more political than economic in nature. The same appears to be true in Aristotle's account of the *stasis* that led to the revolt of Mytilene. On the death of Timophanes, a well-to-do citizen, Dexitheos, proxenos of Athens, was disappointed in his expectation to obtain Timophanes' two heiresses as wives for his sons; consequently, he fomented *stasis* and invited Athenian intervention.[190] Since Dexitheos was

---

[188] IV. 8, 1293b36–40: ... τὰς δὲ πρὸς τὴν ὀλιγαρχίαν (sc. ἀποκλινούσας) μᾶλλον ἀριστοκρατίας διὰ τὸ μᾶλλον ἀκολουθεῖν παιδείαν καὶ εὐγένειαν τοῖς εὐπορωτέροις. ἔτι δὲ δοκοῦσιν ἔχειν οἱ εὔποροι ὧν ἕνεκεν οἱ ἀδικοῦντες ἀδικοῦσιν· ὅθεν καὶ καλοὺς κἀγαθοὺς καὶ γνωρίμους τούτους προσαγορεύουσιν.

[189] V. 4, 1303b34–7: ὁ μὲν γὰρ ἀπορώτερος, ὡς οὐκ ἀποφαίνοντος τὴν οὐσίαν οὐδὲ τὸν θησαυρὸν ὃν εὗρεν ὁ πατήρ, προσήγετο τοὺς δημοτικούς, ὁ δ' ἕτερος ἔχων οὐσίαν πολλὴν τοὺς εὐπόρους.

[190] Ibid. 1304a4–10: καὶ περὶ Μυτιλήνην δὲ ἐξ ἐπικλήρων στάσεως γενομένης πολλῶν ἐγένετο ἀρχὴ κακῶν καὶ τοῦ πολέμου τοῦ πρὸς Ἀθηναίους, ἐν ᾧ Πάχης ἔλαβε τὴν πόλιν αὐτῶν· Τιμοφάνους γὰρ τῶν εὐπόρων τινὸς καταλιπόντος δύο

socially prominent enough to be proxenos of Athens, he will have been no less εὔπορος than Timophanes had been: there is no ἄπορος in this story.[191] Again, a personal dispute involving property had political consequences.

When discussing the economic aspects of the origin of some tyrannies, too, Aristotle speaks of the "wealthy" rather than of the "well-to-do" as the objects of popular resentment. Peisistratus, for example, built his following on hatred of the wealthy (τῶν πλουσίων) current among the common people of Athens; Dionysius was confirmed as tyrant of Syracuse when he had successfully prosecuted Daphnaeus and the wealthy; only in the case of Theagenes of Megara are the opponents whose herds he slaughtered called εὔποροι (V. 5, 1305a21–8), because it is their political status, not their wealth that he was after. In the cases of Peisistratus and Dionysius the aim of popular resentment was not the social status of the upper class but their excessive wealth; in the case of Theagenes it was social and political standing derived from wealth.

Similar motivations for changing the constitution rather than overthrowing it in favour of tyranny are also attributed to oligarchs who, having wasted their fortunes through loose living, call in foreign settlers with whose help they try to dislodge the well-to-do, presumably to take power into their own hands (V. 6, 1306a2–4). More purely politically motivated is oligarchical *stasis* among εὔποροι who have been excluded from office through regulations limiting eligibility to a very small number (e.g., when tenure of office by a father precludes his sons from holding office) (V. 6, 1305b1–10).

Stasis frequently develops when the gulf between the well-to-do and the indigent becomes too wide (ὅταν οἱ μὲν ἀπορῶσι λίαν οἱ δ' εὐπορῶσι), as was the case in Sparta at the time of the Messenian War, which reduced some people to such straits that they demanded a redistribution of land (V. 7, 1306b36–1307a2). These are obviously circumstances in which the issue goes beyond wealth and poverty: survival or starvation are at stake. The stability of states depends, therefore, *inter alia*, on maintaining a balance between εὔποροι and ἄποροι; the domination of one or the other will induce changes in the constitution to reflect the special interests of the dominant group. Where the well-to-do dominate, their arrogance and greed

---

θυγατέρας, ὁ περιωσθεὶς καὶ οὐ λαβὼν τοῖς υἱέσιν αὐτοῦ Δέξανδρος ἦρξε τῆς στάσεως καὶ τοὺς Ἀθηναίους παρώξυνε, πρόξενος ὢν τῆς πόλεως. There is no necessary conflict between this account of the origin of the Mytilenean Revolt of 428/7 B.C.E. and that given by Thucydides at III. 2–6 and 8–18. The difference is merely that Thucydides makes no mention of the personal element.

[191] Note that in Thucydides' version (III. 27) it is the ἀπορία of the δῆμος (though not called by that name) that precipitates the revolt.

d. "Well-to-do" and "indigent" in oligarchy and democracy

will make for change of one sort; where the more indigent dominate, their sense of being treated unjustly makes for change of another sort: thus polities can become democracies and aristocracies oligarchies, or aristocracies democracies and polities oligarchies (V. 7, 1307a19–27). The fact that elsewhere in the *Politics* (IV. 12, 1297a11–12) the wealthy are blamed for ruining the state through their greed suggests that the οἱ ἐν ταῖς εὐπορίαις – the well-to-do – in the present passage are identical with them; but if so, their description as οἱ ἐν ταῖς εὐπορίαις may suggest that wealth is not the only – and perhaps not even the dominant – characteristic of this group: the status and prestige that give them power and influence, denying it to the ἀπορώτεροι, may play a more important part.

Aristotle's account of how a balance between well-to-do and indigent can be established and maintained is so central to Aristotle's political thinking that it is worth quoting it in full:

> The most important thing in every constitution is to create through the enactment of laws and general administration a system that will make it impossible for the magistrates to enrich themselves through their tenure of office. Cautionary measures are especially important in oligarchical governments. For the masses are less resentful of their own ineligibility to office – in fact, they welcome being left the leisure to pursue their own personal affairs – than of the thought that the magistrates are embezzling public funds. That irks them in two ways: (1) in that they are excluded from the prestige of office, and (2) that they cannot enrich themselves through office. Moreover, if there is a possibility of bringing about a democracy that is also an aristocracy, this is it. In this way, too, the upper class and the masses can implement what both desire, namely the realization of the democratic principle that the right to hold office is open to all, and of the aristocratic principle that the élite should hold office.
>
> That goal can be attained only when it is impossible to make profit from public office: the indigent (ἄποροι) will not want to hold office, because it brings no profit, and will rather turn to their own affairs, while the well-to-do (εὔποροι) will be able to hold office because they need no public subvention. The result will be that the indigent become well-to-do by devoting themselves to their business, while the upper class will not be ruled by just anybody.
>
> To prevent embezzlement of public funds, the transfer of funds from outgoing to incoming officials should take place in the presence of the entire citizenry, and copies of the relevant documents should be deposited in each phratry, army-unit, and tribe. Honours established by law should be conferred upon those who have distinguished themselves by

making no profit from their magistracies. Moreover, in democracies the well-to-do should be treated with consideration; not only their properties but also their produce, which under some constitutions is at present gradually and imperceptibly eroded by distributions, should be protected against redistribution. Better still, even if they are willing, they should not be made to perform costly but useless liturgies, such as underwriting choruses, torch-races, and that sort of thing. In oligarchies, a great deal of attention should be paid to the indigent: they should be assigned magistracies that carry fringe benefits, and if any of the well-to-do treat them in a humiliating way, the penalties should be more severe than if the offender had humiliated one of his own kind. Inheritance should not be by bequest but by title of descent, and not more than one inheritance should go to any one person. In this way, the size of estates would be more equitable and a greater number of indigent persons would become well-to-do.

It is also good policy in a democracy as well as in an oligarchy to treat those disadvantaged by the political system with equal or even higher consideration—in a democracy the well-to-do and in an oligarchy the indigent, except that the sovereign organs of the constitution must be entrusted exclusively or for the most part to those who enjoy full constitutional rights.[192]

---

[192] V. 8, 1308b31–1309a32: μέγιστον δὲ ἐν πάσῃ πολιτείᾳ τὸ καὶ τοῖς νόμοις καὶ τῇ ἄλλῃ οἰκονομίᾳ οὕτω τετάχθαι ὥστε μὴ εἶναι τὰς ἀρχὰς κερδαίνειν. τοῦτο δὲ μάλιστα ἐν ταῖς ὀλιγαρχικαῖς δεῖ τηρεῖν. οὐ γὰρ οὕτως ἀγανακτοῦσιν εἰργόμενοι τοῦ ἄρχειν οἱ πολλοί, ἀλλὰ καὶ χαίρουσιν ἐάν τις ἐᾷ πρὸς τοῖς ἰδίοις σχολάζειν, ὥστ' ἐὰν οἴωνται τὰ κοινὰ κλέπτειν τοὺς ἄρχοντας, τότε γ' ἀμφότερα λυπεῖ, τό τε τῶν τιμῶν μὴ μετέχειν καὶ τὸ τῶν κερδῶν· μοναχῶς δὲ καὶ ἐνδέχεται ἅμα εἶναι δημοκρατίαν καὶ ἀριστοκρατίαν, εἰ τοῦτο κατασκευάσειέ τις. ἐνδέχοιτο γὰρ ἂν καὶ τοὺς γνωρίμους καὶ τὸ πλῆθος ἔχειν ἃ βούλονται ἀμφοτέρους. τὸ μὲν γὰρ ἐξεῖναι πᾶσιν ἄρχειν δημοκρατικόν, τὸ δὲ τοὺς γνωρίμους εἶναι ἐν ταῖς ἀρχαῖς ἀριστοκρατικόν, τοῦτο δ' ἔσται ὅταν μὴ ᾖ κερδαίνειν ἀπὸ τῶν ἀρχῶν· οἱ γὰρ ἄποροι οὐ βουλήσονται ἄρχειν τῷ μηδὲν κερδαίνειν, ἀλλὰ πρὸς τοῖς ἰδίοις εἶναι μᾶλλον, οἱ δὲ εὔποροι δυνήσονται διὰ τὸ μηδενὸς προσδεῖσθαι τῶν κοινῶν· ὥστε συμβήσεται τοῖς μὲν ἀπόροις γίγνεσθαι εὐπόροις διὰ τὸ διατρίβειν πρὸς τοῖς ἔργοις, τοῖς δὲ γνωρίμοις μὴ ἄρχεσθαι ὑπὸ τῶν τυχόντων. τοῦ μὲν οὖν μὴ κλέπτεσθαι τὰ κοινὰ ἡ παράδοσις γιγνέσθω τῶν χρημάτων παρόντων πάντων τῶν πολιτῶν, καὶ ἀντίγραφα κατὰ τὰς φατρίας καὶ λόχους καὶ φυλὰς τιθέσθωσαν· τοῦ δὲ ἀκερδῶς ἄρχειν τιμὰς εἶναι δεῖ νενομοθετημένας τοῖς εὐδοκιμοῦσιν. δεῖ δ' ἐν μὲν ταῖς δημοκρατίαις τῶν εὐπόρων φείδεσθαι, μὴ μόνον τῷ τὰς κτήσεις μὴ ποιεῖν ἀναδάστους, ἀλλὰ μηδὲ τοὺς καρπούς, ὃ ἐν ἐνίαις τῶν πολιτειῶν λανθάνει γιγνόμενον, βέλτιον δὲ καὶ βουλομένους κωλύειν λειτουργεῖν τὰς δαπανηρὰς μὲν μὴ χρησίμους δὲ λειτουργίας, οἷον χορηγίας καὶ λαμπαδαρχίας καὶ ὅσαι ἄλλαι τοιαῦται· ἐν δ' ὀλιγαρχίᾳ τῶν ἀπόρων ἐπιμέλειαν ποιεῖσθαι πολλήν, καὶ τὰς ἀρχὰς ἀφ' ὧν λήμματα <ἔστι> τούτοις ἀπονέμειν, κἂν τις ὑβρίσῃ τῶν εὐπόρων εἰς τούτους, μείζω τὰ ἐπιτίμια εἶναι ἢ ἂν σφῶν αὐτῶν, καὶ

d. "Well-to-do" and "indigent" in oligarchy and democracy

It is, in my opinion, significant that the terms πλούσιος, πένης, and their cognates are conspicuously absent from this passage. The description of good government as precluding the possibility of embezzlement by public officials and as subjecting the funds they administer to the scrutiny of the entire citizen body envisions a citizen who regards the value of wealth as consisting exclusively in providing the wherewithal to serve the community. The ἄποροι are to be given every opportunity to enhance their economic status to the point of becoming themselves εὔποροι; they are not to threaten those better off than themselves with redistribution of property; those offices from which legitimate benefits can be derived will be assigned to them: all this points to a society in which it is not a distinction between wealth and poverty that determines the character of government, but in which both economic groups serve the interests of the community with mutual respect and to the best of their ability. It is, indeed, as Aristotle puts it, a democracy that is at the same time an aristocracy, perhaps in a sense similar to the idealization in John F. Kennedy's inaugural speech: "ask not what your country can do for you, ask what you can do for your country."

There is no context in which being well-to-do and being indigent figure more prominently or are more prominently linked to wealth and poverty than Aristotle's discussion of democracy and oligarchy. The fact that these two régimes are deviations (παρεκβάσεις) from the correct forms of government, which envisage the interest of the community as a whole, and are governed in the interest of the rulers,[193] explains why an oligarchy is defined as aiming at "the interest of" the well-to-do (εὔποροι) and a democracy as that of the indigent (ἄποροι).[194] The interest of the well-to-do and of the indigent, respectively, are thus the essential differentiae between

---

τὰς κληρονομίας μὴ κατὰ δόσιν εἶναι ἀλλὰ κατὰ γένος, μηδὲ πλειόνων ἢ μιᾶς τὸν αὐτὸν κληρονομεῖν. οὕτω γὰρ ἂν ὁμαλώτεραι αἱ οὐσίαι εἶεν καὶ τῶν ἀπόρων εἰς εὐπορίαν ἂν καθίσταιντο πλείους. συμφέρει δὲ καὶ ἐν δημοκρατίᾳ καὶ ἐν ὀλιγαρχίᾳ τῶν ἄλλων ἢ ἰσότητα ἢ προεδρίαν νέμειν τοῖς ἧττον κοινωνοῦσι τῆς πολιτείας, ἐν μὲν δήμῳ τοῖς εὐπόροις, ἐν δ' ὀλιγαρχίᾳ τοῖς ἀπόροις, πλὴν ὅσαι ἀρχαὶ κύριαι τῆς πολιτείας, ταύτας δὲ τοῖς ἐκ τῆς πολιτείας ἐγχειρίζειν μόνοις ἢ πλείοσιν.

[193] III. 7, 1279a25–31. The relevant phrases are: πρὸς τὸ κοινὸν συμφέρον as contrasted with πρὸς τὸ ἴδιον ἢ τοῦ ἑνὸς ἢ τῶν ὀλίγων ἢ τοῦ πλήθους (συμφέρον).

[194] Ibid. 1279b7–10: ... ἡ δ' ὀλιγαρχία πρὸς τὸ τῶν εὐπόρων (συμφέρον), ἡ δὲ δημοκρατία πρὸς τὸ συμφέρον τὸ τῶν ἀπόρων· πρὸς δὲ τὸ τῷ κοινῷ λυσιτελοῦν οὐδεμία αὐτῶν. Cf. Pericles' definition at Thuc. II. 37. 1: καὶ ὄνομα μὲν διὰ τὸ μὴ ἐς ὀλίγους ἀλλ' ἐς πλείονας οἰκεῖν δημοκρατία κέκληται. It is curious to note how much more prominently the interest group figures in Greek definitions of constitutions than it does, for example in Lincoln's famous definition of democracy as government of, for and by the people. Cf. Salkever (1991) 13: "decisions are motivated by the desire to improve the lives of all the citizens."

oligarchy and democracy. The conventional quantitative differentiae are decidedly secondary: whether it is a rule of the few or of the many, of a minority or of a majority is, in Aristotle's view, merely accidental.[195] Quantitative considerations do, however, enter in the amount of property required for eligibility to office in these two constitutional systems: both take ownership of property for granted as a prerequisite for eligibility; but while in an oligarchy "those who own estates" (οἱ τὰς οὐσίας ἔχοντες) dominate, the ἄποροι rulers of a democracy are defined as those "who do not possess *considerable* estates" (οἱ μὴ κεκτημένοι πλῆθος οὐσίας) (1279b17–19). We have seen above what kind of property constitutes οὐσία for Aristotle and how it differs from those kinds of property that he terms κτῆσις or κτήματα.[196] The question that concerns us here is the precise relation between εὐπορία and πλοῦτος and between ἀπορία and πενία, or in short, the question whether the presence of material assets alone constitutes affluence and their absence indigence.

Although Aristotle often describes an oligarchy indifferently in terms of dominance by either the εὔποροι or the πλούσιοι, and a democracy in terms of dominance by either the ἄποροι or the πένητες,[197] there are a number of unequivocal signs that he regards the pairs as no more identical in the context of oligarchy-democracy than he does in the other contexts we have examined. One telling passage condemns as equally unjust both the democratic and the oligarchical views of equality: the oligarchical view, which regards the decisions of owners of larger estates to be just, is condemned on the grounds that it would justify a tyranny if one person should own more property than all the other well-to-do (εὔποροι) combined;[198] the populist view that the decisions of the majority are just is condemned because it would justify their confiscation of the property of the wealthy minority (τῶν πλουσίων καὶ ἐλαττόνων).[199] The use of εὔποροι in this context indicates that the larger possessions of the tyrant do not give him any more εὐπορία to govern than those who have less than he; at the same time, in democracies it is the πλοῦτος of the upper class that can be expropriated, but they cannot be deprived of their εὐπορία, inasmuch as their fitness for office is not in question. The point seems corroborated by the statement that in an oligarchy only εὔποροι are eligible for office

---

[195] See III. 8, 1279b11–1280a6; and IV. 4, 1290a30–b3 with p. 43 and n. 113 above.
[196] See above, pp. 44–49.
[197] III. 8, 1279b39–1280b6; IV. 4, 1290a33–b3.
[198] VI. 3, 1318a23–4: ἐὰν εἷς ἔχῃ πλείω τῶν ἄλλων εὐπόρων, κατὰ τὸ ὀλιγαρχικὸν δίκαιον ἄρχειν δίκαιος μόνος.
[199] Ibid. 24–6: εἰ δ' ὅ τι ἂν οἱ πλείους κατ' ἀριθμόν, ἀδικήσουσι δημεύοντες τὰ τῶν πλουσίων καὶ ἐλαττόνων.

d. "Well-to-do" and "indigent" in oligarchy and democracy

despite their small number, and that in a democracy ἄποροι are eligible because of their large number.[200] It is not wealth that makes a person eligible for office in an oligarchy but assets sufficient to enable him not to have to work for a living; it is not poverty that is a bar to eligibility in a democracy, nor is, for that matter, the lack of sufficient assets, since, we may assume, pay for office (μισθός) makes up for that lack. This explains also why in the "first" type of democracy, which is based on equality, neither the indigent nor the well-to-do dominate: since neither have greater prominence, sovereignty cannot be defined in terms of either group.[201]

That the wealthy may dominate in an oligarchy not by reason of their wealth but because of the εὐπορία through which wealth makes them fit to rule and to hold office also emerges from an examination of the vocabulary used to show how elements in democracy and oligarchy can be fused into the formation of a polity. The oligarchical method of compelling the εὔποροι to serve as jurors by penalizing them for non-attendance and of not encouraging the ἄποροι by paying them to attend is to be combined with the democratic device of pay for the ἄποροι but no penalties for the εὔποροι (IV. 9, 1294a37–41). There is no talk here of πλούσιοι and πένητες, because the issue is participation in the judicial process as a function of citizenship, that is, on a political rather than on an economic basis.[202]

One of the reasons for the stability of a polity is that it is a blend of εὔποροι and ἄποροι and at the same time of wealth and freedom (IV. 8, 1294a16–19), that is, it includes both those who have the material preconditions for active participation in public affairs and those who have not; wealth is the asset of one group, freedom the asset of all, including those citizens who are materially disadvantaged. Moreover, it is a mean between the "very well-to-do" (εὔποροι σφόδρα) and the "very indigent" (ἄποροι σφόδρα), and its strength resides in being vested in a middle class (IV. 11, 1295b1–3). The rarity of a middle class is given as a reason why most states are either democracies or oligarchies: where the indigent dominate there will be democracy, and where the well-to-do and prominent dominate oligarchy (IV. 12, 1296b24–34, cf. VI. 2, 1317b8–10). The tone of each is

---

[200] III. 8, 1279b28–31, cf. nn. 109 and 113 above.

[201] IV. 4, 1291b30–4: δημοκρατία μὲν οὖν ἐστι πρώτη ἡ μὲν λεγομένη μάλιστα κατὰ τὸ ἴσον. ἴσον γάρ φησιν ὁ νόμος ὁ τῆς τοιαύτης δημοκρατίας τὸ μηδὲν μᾶλλον ὑπερέχειν τοὺς ἀπόρους ἢ τοὺς εὐπόρους, μηδὲ κυρίους εἶναι ὁποτερουσοῦν, ἀλλ' ὁμοίους ἀμφοτέρους. See also the definition of the principle of numerical equality at VI. 2, 1318a6–8: ἴσον γὰρ τὸ μηδὲν μᾶλλον ἄρχειν τοὺς ἀπόρους ἢ τοὺς εὐπόρους, μηδὲ κυρίους εἶναι μόνους ἀλλὰ πάντας ἐξ ἴσου κατ' ἀριθμόν.

[202] For discussions of related issues exclusively in terms of εὔποροι and ἄποροι without mention of πλούσιοι and πένητες, see IV. 13, 1297a14–b1, and VI. 5, 1320a 24–b4.

set by social and political rather than by purely economic factors. This is indicated also by the fact that *stasis* may have its origin in the contempt of the well-to-do for the indiscipline and anarchy (τῆς ἀταξίας καὶ ἀναρχίας) rampant in a democracy (V. 3, 1302b25–9): their discontent is based not on their wealth but on their social status. Conversely, when *stasis* consists of an attack by the common people on the well-to-do, the use of εὔποροι suggests that political clout rather than wealth is the ground for conflict (IV. 11, 1296a27–32).

Finally, there is Aristotle's criticism of Plato's analysis of the causes of political change in *Republic* VIII. In objecting to Plato's statement that an oligarchical state is split into two, a state of the wealthy and a state of the poor, Aristotle argues that "states change from oligarchy to democracy without anyone having become poorer than before, if the indigent (οἱ ἄποροι) increase in number, and from democracy to oligarchy if the well-to-do (τὸ εὔπορον) become superior to the masses, while one side is indifferent and the other vigilant."[203] We have here another clear statement of Aristotle's conviction that factors other than wealth and poverty differentiate an oligarchy from a democracy: it is partly a matter of numbers (πλείους) and partly a matter of superior influence (κρεῖττον) that is decisive.[204] For our definition of oligarchy we may conclude from this that while the wealthy dominate in oligarchies, their political strength derives from a number of factors, the sum of which constitutes their εὐπορία. Wealth is likely to be one of them, but it is not the only one. What characterizes them is that they do not require public subventions to be able to govern, since their private resources provide them with a sufficient income to enable them to devote themselves to public affairs. In a democracy, on the other hand, the possession of private resources is not the decisive factor for participating in an active political life: the state is willing to supplement by pay the income of the indigent to enable them to exercise their rights as citizens.

---

[203] V. 12, 1316b6–14: ἄτοπον δὲ καὶ τὸ φάναι δύο πόλεις εἶναι τὴν ὀλιγαρχικήν, πλουσίων καὶ πενήτων, οὐδενὸς δὲ πενεστέρου γενομένου ἢ πρότερον οὐδὲν ἧττον μεταβάλλουσιν εἰς δῆμον ἐξ ὀλιγαρχίας, ἂν γένωνται πλείους οἱ ἄποροι, καὶ ἐκ δήμου εἰς ὀλιγαρχίαν, ἐὰν κρεῖττον ᾖ τοῦ πλήθους τὸ εὔπορον καὶ οἱ μὲν ἀμελῶσιν οἱ δὲ προσέχωσι τὸν νοῦν.

[204] For a similar statement, see V. 3, where change in constitutions is attributed to an increase in size, at 1303a1–2 of τὸ ἀπόρων πλῆθος in democracies and polities, and at 1303a10–13 πλειόνων γὰρ τῶν εὐπόρων γινομένων ἢ τῶν οὐσιῶν αὐξανομένων μεταβάλλουσιν εἰς ὀλιγαρχίας καὶ δυναστείας. Again, wealth or poverty are not the sole decisive factors.

E. OLIGARCHICAL WEALTH AND PUBLIC SERVICE

The ownership of a large amount of property constitutes wealth, and since by its very nature "wealth" (πλοῦτος) gives a person the resources (εὐπορία) to exercise active citizenship, both in qualifying him to vote and in making him eligible to hold office, wealth becomes a precondition for active citizenship in oligarchies.[205] It is by reason of their wealth (διὰ πλοῦτον) that oligarchs rule;[206] it is wealth that defines oligarchy;[207] and to be wealthy means *ipso facto* to be εὔπορος, that is, to have the private resources that enable a person to devote himself to public affairs, especially in an oligarchy,[208] where authority rests in the hands of those who own estates,[209] and who rule in the interest of the well-to-do (εὔποροι).[210] This entails a higher social standing; they are bracketed with the upper social class (καλοὶ κἀγαθοί, γνώριμοι), and they are the *hommes de qualité*.[211]

The degree to which an oligarchy admitted a person to participation in the life of the community depended on the amount of property he owned, as established by his τίμημα. A minimal valuation was required for basic citizenship, that is, the right to vote and to elect;[212] θῆτες were admitted, βάναυσοι not.[213] Eligibility to office was predicated on wealth,[214] and its amount, as established by a τίμημα,[215] was a determining factor in eligibility to deliberative, judicial, and executive office.[216] Laws stipulated the amount of property required for admission to the various civic activities.[217] The τιμήματα were large enough to exclude ἄποροι from participation in public affairs altogether.[218] A low τίμημα secured admission to member-

---

[205] Arist., *Pol.* IV. 4, 1290a30–b3; 8, 1294a11.
[206] Ibid. III. 8, 1280a1–2; cf. πλουτίνδην at II.11, 1273a26.
[207] Ibid. IV. 8, 1294a11: ὅρος... ὀλιγαρχίας δὲ πλοῦτος.
[208] Ibid. IV. 4, 1291b7–13.
[209] Ibid. III. 8, 1279b17–18: οἱ τὰς οὐσίας ἔχοντες; cf. VI. 3, 1318a20, where their values (τὸ δίκαιον) are described as those of an oligarchy.
[210] Ibid. III. 7, 1279b8.
[211] Ibid. IV. 8, 1294a18–19, 1293b41–42; see esp. 12, 1296b31–33: ὅπου δὲ τὸ τῶν εὐπόρων καὶ γνωρίμων μᾶλλον ὑπερτείνει τῷ ποιῷ ἢ λείπεται τῷ ποσῷ, ἐνταῦθα ὀλιγαρχίαν.... Cf. also IV. 4, 1290b20 and VI. 2, 1317b38–41.
[212] Ibid. IV. 6, 1292b31–33.
[213] Ibid. III. 5, 1278a21–25.
[214] Ibid., II. 11, 1273a25–26; IV. 15, 1299b25–26.
[215] Ibid., IV. 9, 1294b10; III. 5, 1278a24.
[216] Ibid. V. 6, 1306b8–9.
[217] Ibid. IV. 6, 1292b29–30.
[218] Ibid. IV. 5, 1292a39–40.

ship in the assembly, the council, and the jury courts,[219] a higher for any public office.[220] The highest public officials, such as generals and treasurers, were selected from the highest property classes.[221]

Some further oligarchical characteristics emerge from Aristotle's comparisons of oligarchical with democratic practices. All these are geared to establishing and maintaining the limitations that a government by and for a limited social and economic group entails. While in a democracy many officials are chosen by lot, in an oligarchy the direct election of magistrates ensures the exclusion of economically unqualified persons, the indigent. Once in office their rule is stricter and more authoritarian than it is in a democracy:[222] more rigorous rules of public conduct are enforced: attendance at assembly meetings and participation in electing public officials is compulsory for oligarchical citizens[223] and failure to do so results in fines.[224] Propertied citizens are not permitted to decline public office, and the well-to-do cannot refuse jury duty, while the indigent can.[225] Two features mentioned as oligarchical elements of the Spartan constitution are (a) the powerful *pentarchia* constituted by co-option and given the right of appointing the the highest officials, the *One Hundred*, and (b) a longer tenure of office than the rest.[226]

In short, in order to protect its integrity as government by the propertied classes, an oligarchy has to insist on participation in public affairs more rigorously than does a democracy.

F. THE FOUR KINDS OF OLIGARCHY

On the basis of the three criteria of size of property (οὐσία), property assessment (τίμημα), and participation in decision-making, Aristotle distinguishes four types of oligarchy. These are, in increasing order of narrowness:[227]

---

[219] Ibid. III. 11, 1282a29–31; cf. V. 6, 1306b7–9. Note that no (or only a low) τίμημα was prerequisite for admission to office in democracies, IV. 4, 1291b39–40; VI. 2, 1317b22–23.
[220] Ibid. III. 5, 1278a23; IV. 5, 1292b1.
[221] Ibid. II. 6, 1266a13–14; VI. 6, 1320b21–24; and esp. III. 11, 1282a31–32.
[222] Ibid. IV. 9, 1294b8–9; 3, 1290a27–29.
[223] Ibid. IV. 13, 1297a17–19.
[224] Ibid. II. 6, 1266a9–10.
[225] Ibid. IV. 13, 1297a19–22; cf. 9, 1294a37–41.
[226] Ibid. II. 11, 1273a13–17.
[227] On the classification in general, see ibid. VI. 6, 1320b18–33.

(1) A state in which many own each a small amount of property, just large enough not be rated as indigent; since their number is large and many enjoy citizenship, laws rather than men are sovereign.[228]
(2) The laws are also sovereign in the second kind of oligarchy, in which a high property assessment is required both of the electorate and of those eligible for office, who observe the law in making their decisions.[229]
(3) The third kind also adheres to the laws but has a still higher property qualification. In addition, a law enforces the hereditary feature that son succeeds father by co-option.[230]
(4) The narrowest kind of oligarchy is more properly called a "clique" (δυναστεία), in which wealth and a network of relationships are the self-perpetuating constitutive factor; it is a rule of men and not of laws.[231]

G. CONCLUSION: OLIGARCHICAL CITIZENSHIP

We have seen that in Aristotle's view the possession of a minimum of property is required in all actual constitutions even of the most insignificant citizen. His statement that those whom poverty makes ineligible for office will peacefully accept exclusion from the political process as long as they are not subjected to violence and not deprived of any of their property suggests that they own at least some property (IV. 13, 1297b6–8). A situation of this kind is likely to prevail in states in which manual laborers predominate, who "have so little property that they are unable to enjoy the leisure" <needed to engage in public affairs>.[232] It will also prevail in the agricultural type of democracy, dominated by "people of moderate property ... whose livelihood depends on their working without enjoyment of leisure, so that they make the law supreme and hold no more Assembly meetings than necessary."[233] But, Aristotle adds, those who do not belong to this class get full citizen rights "as soon as they have attained the property qualification (τίμημα) specified by the laws; therefore all property owners

---

[228] Ibid. IV. 5, 1292a29–41; 6, 1293a13–20; 14, 1298a35–40.
[229] Ibid. IV. 5, 1292b1–4; 6, 1293a21–26; 14, 1298a40–b2.
[230] Ibid. IV. 9, 1294b4–5; 6, 1293a26–30; 14, 1298b2–5.
[231] Ibid. IV. 5, 1292b5–7; 6, 1293a30–32.
[232] IV. 4, 1291b25–26: τὸ χερνητικὸν καὶ τὸ μικρὰν ἔχον οὐσίαν ὥστε μὴ δύνασθαι σχολάζειν.
[233] Ibid. 6, 1292b25–29: τὸ γεωργικὸν καὶ τὸ κεκτημένον μετρίαν οὐσίαν... (ἔχουσι γὰρ ἐργαζόμενοι ζῆν, οὐ δύνανται δὲ σχολάζειν, ὥστε τὸν νόμον ἐπιστήσαντες ἐκκλησιάζουσι τὰς ἀναγκαίας ἐκκλησίας).

are entitled to share in the state."[234] In short, some measure of εὐπορία is required for any kind of participation in public affairs, but the degree of participation depends on the size of the property a given person owns.

The best government is one in which the politically active population consists of owners of moderate and sufficient property (οὐσίαν μέσην καὶ ἱκανήν) (IV. 11, 1295b39–40), and equality of estates (τὸ τὰς οὐσίας ἴσας εἶναι) is recommended internally as inhibiting civil conflict (II. 7, 1267a37–b9). But governments of this sort are rare. As the number of well-to-do or the size of estates increases, more or less narrow oligarchies develop,[235] and with it opposition between property-owners (οἱ τὰς οὐσίας ἔχοντες) and the common people (δῆμος) (IV. 11, 1296a25) begins to raise its head. The key text is: "an oligarchy exists when the owners of estates control the constitutional authority in the state; a democracy, conversely, when the indigent (ἄποροι) who do not own a sizable estate are in control."[236] An oligarchy admits only εὔποροι to citizenship;[237] ἄποροι, whose numbers give them power, can enjoy full citizenship only in a democracy, not in an oligarchy.[238] Ancient Colophon is defined as an oligarchy, despite the fact that the owners of large estates constituted the majority of its citizens (IV. 4, 1290b15–17), before their defeat by the Lydians.[239]

The ownership of a large amount of property constitutes wealth, and since by its very nature "wealth" (πλοῦτος) gives a person the resources (εὐπορία) to exercise active citizenship, it becomes a precondition for active citizenship in oligarchies.[240] It is by reason of their wealth (διὰ πλοῦτον) that oligarchs rule;[241] it is wealth that defines oligarchy;[242] and to be wealthy means *ipso facto* to be εὔπορος, that is, to have the private resources that enable a person to devote himself to public affairs, especially in an oligarchy,[243] where authority rests in the hands of those who own

---

[234] Ibid. 29–31: τοῖς δὲ ἄλλοις μετέχειν ἔξεστιν ὅταν κτήσωνται τὸ τίμημα τὸ διωρισμένον ὑπὸ τῶν νόμων· διὸ πᾶσι τοῖς κτησαμένοις ἔξεστι μετέχειν.

[235] V. 3, 1303a11–13: πλειόνων γὰρ τῶν εὐπόρων γινομένων ἢ τῶν οὐσιῶν αὐξανομένων μεταβάλλουσιν εἰς ὀλιγαρχίας καὶ δυναστείας.

[236] Ibid. III. 8, 1279b17–19: ...ὀλιγαρχία δ' ὅταν ὦσι κύριοι τῆς πολιτείας οἱ τὰς οὐσίας ἔχοντες, δημοκρατία δὲ τοὐναντίον ὅταν οἱ μὴ κεκτημένοι πλῆθος οὐσίας ἀλλ' ἄποροι. See p. 60 above.

[237] See p. 67 above.

[238] See above, pp. 59–60.

[239] This probably refers to Colophon's defeat by Gyges in the first half of the seventh century B.C.E. (see Hdt. I. 14 .4).

[240] Arist., *Pol.* IV. 4, 1290a30–b3; 8, 1294a11.

[241] Ibid. III. 8, 1280a1–2; cf. πλουτίνδην at II.11, 1273a26.

[242] Ibid. IV. 8, 1294a11: ὅρος... ὀλιγαρχίας δὲ πλοῦτος.

[243] Ibid. IV. 4, 1291b7–13.

g. Conclusion: Oligarchical citizenship

estates.²⁴⁴ A further mark of oligarchy is that it is ruled in the interest of the well-to-do (εὔποροι).²⁴⁵ Moreover, since oligarchical moral standards give precedence to the decisions of rich landowners,²⁴⁶ the rich enjoy a higher social standing; they are bracketed with the upper social class (καλοὶ κἀγαθοί, γνώριμοι), and they are the social élite.²⁴⁷

Ownership of property is the basis of all of the four types of oligarchy he recognizes. The passage is worth quoting it in full, especially since it works up to a differentiation of a narrow power-group from an oligarchy (δυναστεία, ὀλιγαρχία).

> As for oligarchy: when a greater number of people own estates of smaller and not excessive size, we have the first type of oligarchy. They permit a property-owner to be a member, and, with a large number of men having a share in governing, authority will necessarily be vested not in men but in the law. For the further removed they are from monarchy, <the less likely it will be that> their estate will either be so large that they can enjoy leisure without concern for their their property, or so small that they have to be maintained from city funds. It follows that they think it right that the law should rule over them and not they.
>
> When the number of estate owners is smaller but their estates larger, we get the second type of oligarchy. Their greater influence, they believe, entitles them to greater prerogatives. Accordingly, they take it upon themselves to chose from the rest those who will be admitted to the governing body; but since they are not quite influential enough to rule without law, they enact a law to that effect.
>
> If they narrow it by having fewer people own larger estates, the third stage of oligarchy is reached. They keep the offices in their own hands but adopt a law stipulating that sons succeed their fathers. When they confine <membership> to an extreme extent requiring <large> estates limited to a network of relationships, we have a narrow power-group (δυναστεία) which is close to monarchy, in which authority rests with men and not with law. This is the fourth type of oligarchy, the counterpart to the final kind of democracy.²⁴⁸

---

²⁴⁴ Ibid. III. 8, 1279b17–18, as cited on p. 66 above.
²⁴⁵ Ibid. III. 7, 1279b8. See above, p. 69 with n. 210.
²⁴⁶ See above, p. 69 with n. 209.
²⁴⁷ Ibid. IV. 8, 1294a18–19, 1293b41–42; see esp. 12, 1296b31–33: ὅπου δὲ τὸ τῶν εὐπόρων καὶ γνωρίμων μᾶλλον ὑπερτείνει τῷ ποιῷ ἢ λείπεται τῷ ποσῷ, ἐνταῦθα ὀλιγαρχίαν.... Cf. pp. 68–69 above.
²⁴⁸ IV. 6, 1293a12–34: τάδε δὲ τῆς ὀλιγαρχίας· ὅταν μὲν πλείους ἔχωσιν οὐσίαν, ἐλάττω δὲ καὶ μὴ πολλὴν λίαν, τὸ τῆς πρώτης ὀλιγαρχίας εἶδός ἐστιν· ποιοῦσι γὰρ ἐξουσίαν μετέχειν τῷ κτωμένῳ, καὶ διὰ τὸ πλῆθος εἶναι τῶν μετεχόντων τοῦ

This passage shows how the nature of a given oligarchy is determined by the extent of property owned by members of the group admitted to public office; ownership of property itself is taken for granted as it is even in a democracy. The point is corroborated by the oligarchical view of right and wrong. One of the reasons why oligarchical revolutions occur is that those whose estates far exceed those of others do not regard it as right (δίκαιον) that propertied and unpropertied people should have the same share in the city,[249] and that greater assets should give a greater voice in decision-making.[250] But they also tend to make the mistake of assuming that their inequality in terms of their estates makes them unequal (i.e., superior) also in all other respects (V. 1, 1301a31–33).

Participation in public affairs is predicated on the ownership of some – presumably landed – property (οὐσία),[251] it is the amount that matters for admission to its exercise. An "indigent" person, an ἄπορος, is not one who is down-and-out, but one who owns enough property for subsistence to be qualified at least in a democracy to attend important Assembly meetings.[252] The corollary, that the well-to-do (εὔποροι) dominate in an oligarchy, emerges from the subsequent discussion of the problem whether number or wealth determines whether a given state is oligarchical or democratic: "our argument shows that it is accidental that authority lies in the hands of a few

πολιτεύματος ἀνάγκη μὴ τοὺς ἀνθρώπους ἀλλὰ τὸν νόμον εἶναι κύριον (ὅσῳ γὰρ ἂν πλεῖον ἀπέχωσι τῆς μοναρχίας, καὶ μήτε τοσαύτην ἔχωσιν οὐσίαν ὥστε σχολάζειν ἀμελοῦντες, μήθ' οὕτως ὀλίγην ὥστε τρέφεσθαι ἀπὸ τῆς πόλεως, ἀνάγκη τὸν νόμον ἀξιοῦν αὐτοῖς ἄρχειν, ἀλλὰ μὴ αὐτούς)· ἐὰν δὲ ἐλάττους ὦσιν οἱ τὰς οὐσίας ἔχοντες ἢ οἱ τὸ πρότερον, πλείω δέ, τὸ τῆς δευτέρας ὀλιγαρχίας γίνεται εἶδος· μᾶλλον γὰρ ἰσχύοντες πλεονεκτεῖν ἀξιοῦσιν, διὸ αὐτοὶ μὲν αἱροῦνται ἐκ τῶν ἄλλων τοὺς εἰς τὸ πολίτευμα βαδίζοντας, διὰ δὲ τὸ μήπω οὕτως ἰσχυροὶ εἶναι ὥστ' ἄνευ νόμου ἄρχειν τὸν νόμον τίθενται τοιοῦτον. ἐὰν δ' ἐπιτείνωσι τῷ ἐλάττονες ὄντες μείζονας οὐσίας ἔχειν, ἡ τρίτη ἐπίδοσις γίνεται τῆς ὀλιγαρχίας, τὸ δι' αὐτῶν μὲν τὰς ἀρχὰς ἔχειν, κατὰ νόμον δὲ τὸν κελεύοντα διαδέχεσθαι τοὺς υἱεῖς. ὅταν δὲ ἤδη πολὺ ὑπερτείνωσι ταῖς οὐσίαις καὶ ταῖς πολυφιλίαις, ἐγγὺς ἡ τοιαύτη δυναστεία μοναρχίας ἐστίν, καὶ κύριοι γίνονται οἱ ἄνθρωποι, ἀλλ' οὐχ ὁ νόμος· καὶ τὸ τέταρτον εἶδος τῆς ὀλιγαρχίας τοῦτ' ἐστίν, ἀντίστροφον τῷ τελευταίῳ τῆς δημοκρατίας.

[249] V. 12, 1316b1–3: οἱ πολὺ ὑπερέχοντες ταῖς οὐσίαις οὐ δίκαιον οἴονται εἶναι ἴσον μετέχειν τῆς πόλεως τοὺς κεκτημένους μηθὲν τοῖς κεκτημένοις. For a criticism of this view, see above, p. 66 with n. 199.

[250] VI. 3, 1318a20–21: οἱ δ' ὀλιγαρχικοὶ (sc. φασὶ τοῦτο δίκαιον) ὅ τι ἂν δόξῃ τῇ πλείονι οὐσίᾳ· κατὰ πλῆθος γὰρ οὐσίας φασὶ κρίνεσθαι δεῖν.

[251] On the role of land in participation in the community, sc. in citizenship, in Attica, see Link, (1991) 13–43, who, surprisingly ignores Andrewes' chapter on Solon (1982) 377–84. See further above pp. 45–48.

[252] See pp. 55–56 above.

g. Conclusion: Oligarchical citizenship

in oligarchies or of many in democracies, because everywhere the well-to-do are few and the indigent many….The difference between democracy and oligarchy consists in poverty and wealth, respectively: where men rule because of their wealth – whether they are lesser or greater in number – there is oligarchy, and where the indigent rule we have democracy; that the former are fewer and the latter numerous is incidental. For only a few are well-to-do, but all have a share in freedom."[253] It is stated even more explicitly in a later definition of the εὔποροι as those who "perform public service with their οὐσίαι" (IV. 4, 1291a33–34). Where citizenship, i.e., full participation in the affairs of state, including especially eligibility to high office, depend on the ownership of a substantial οὐσία we have oligarchy.

---

[253] III. 8, 1279b34–80a4: ἔοικε τοίνυν ὁ λόγος ποιεῖν δῆλον ὅτι τὸ μὲν ὀλίγους ἢ πολλοὺς εἶναι κυρίους συμβεβηκός ἐστιν, τὸ μὲν ταῖς ὀλιγαρχίαις τὸ δὲ ταῖς δημοκρατίαις, διὰ τὸ τοὺς μὲν εὐπόρους ὀλίγους, πολλοὺς δ' εἶναι τοὺς ἀπόρους πανταχοῦ…, ᾧ δὲ διαφέρουσιν ἥ τε δημοκρατία καὶ ἡ ὀλιγαρχία ἀλλήλων πενία καὶ πλοῦτός ἐστιν, καὶ ἀναγκαῖον μέν, ὅπου ἂν ἄρχωσι διὰ πλοῦτον, ἄν τ' ἐλάττους ἄν τε πλείους, εἶναι ταύτην ὀλιγαρχίαν, ὅπου δ' οἱ ἄποροι, δημοκρατίαν, ἀλλὰ συμβαίνει, καθάπερ εἴπομεν, τοὺς μὲν ὀλίγους εἶναι τοὺς δὲ πολλούς. εὐποροῦσι μὲν γὰρ ὀλίγοι, τῆς δὲ ἐλευθερίας μετέχουσι πάντες.

BIBLIOGRAPHY OF WORKS CITED

Amar, A. R. (1998) *The Bill of Rights: Creation and Reconstruction* (New Haven and London)
Andrewes, A. (1963) *The Greek Tyrants* (New York)
Andrewes, A. (1970) *see under* Gomme, A.W., vol. IV.
Andrewes, A. (1981) *see under* Gomme, A.W., vol. V.
Andrewes, A. (1982) *see under* Gomme, A.W., vol. III. 3.
Anton, J.P. and Kustas, G.L. (edd.) (1971) *Essays in Ancient Greek Philosophy*, (Albany, NY).
Apffel, H. (1957) *Die Verfassungsdebatte bei Herodot (3, 80–82)* (diss. Erlangen)
Asheri, D. (ed.), (1990) *Erodoto: Le storie* III (crit. text by S.M. Medaglia; tr. by A. Frascetti) (Fondazione Lorenzo Valla).
Aubonnet, J. (ed. & tr.) (1971) *Aristote: Politique* II. 1 (Paris).

Barker, E. (1948) *The Politics of Aristotle* (Oxford).
Beloch, J. (1906) "Griechische Aufgebote II," *Klio* 6: 34–78.
Bleicken, J. (1979) "Zur Entstehung der Verfassungstypologie im 5. Jahrhundert v. Chr. (Monarchie, Aristokratie, Demokratie)," *Historia* 28: 48–72.
Böckh, A. (1886) *Die Staatshaushaltung der Athener*, 3rd ed. by Max Fränkel, 2 vols. (Berlin).
Boedeker, D. and Raaflaub, K. (edd.) (1998) *Democracy, Empire, and the Arts in Fifth-Century Athens* (Cambridge & London).
Bordes, J. (1982) *Politeia dans la pensée grecque jusqu'à Aristote* (Paris).
Bowra , C.M. (1964) *Pindar* (Oxford)
Burton, R.W.B. (1962) *Pindar's Pythian Odes* (Oxford).
Busolt, G. and Swoboda, H. (1920–26) *Griechische Staatskunde*. 2 vols (Munich)

Chadwick, J. (1973) "The Linear B Tablets as historical documents," *CAH* II[3], Pt. 1: 609–26.
Cook, J.M. (1982) "The eastern Greeks" in *CAH* III.3[2]: 196–221. .

Davis, R.W. (ed.) (1995) *The Origins of Modern Freedom in the West* (Stanford).
de Romilly, J. (1959) "Le classement des constitutions d'Hérodote à Aristote," *REG* 72: 81–99.
Debrunner, A. (1947) "Δημοκρατία," *Festschrift für Edouard Tièche* (Bern) 11–24.
Dover, K.J. (1970) *see under* Gomme, A.W., vol. IV.
Drews, R. (1983) *Basileus: The Evidence for Kingship in Geometric Greece* (New Haven and London).

Eder, W. (ed.) (1995) *Die athenische Demokratie im 4. Jahrhundert v, Chr.* (Stuttgart)

Ferrill, A. (1978) "Herodotus on tyranny," *Historia* 27: 385–98.

Finley, M.I. (1979) *The World of Odysseus*, 2d ed. (Penguin Books).
Fisher, N.R.E. (1992) *Hybris; A Study in the Values of Honour and Shame in Ancient Greece* (Warminster).
Forsythe, G. *see under* Graham, A.J.

Gammie, J.G. (1986) "Herodotus on kings and tyrants," *JNES* 45: 171–95.
Glassman, R.M. (1986) *Democracy and Despotism in Primitive Societies.* 2 vols. (Millwood, NY,).
Gomme, A.W. (1945–81) with A. Andrewes and K.J. Dover, *A Historical Commentary on Thucydides* (= *HCT*). 5 vols. (Oxford).
Graham, A.J. and Forsythe, G. (1984), "A new slogan for oligarchy in Thucydides III. 82. 8," *HSCP* 88: 25–45.

Harris, E.M. (1992) "Pericles' praise of Athenian democracy: Thucydides 2.37.1," *HSCP* 94: 157–67.
Hölkeskamp, K.-J. (1998) "Parteiungen und die politische Willensbildung im demokratischen Athen: Perikles und Thukydides, Sohn des Melesias," *HZ* 267: 1–27.

Jacobsen, T. (1970a) "Primitive democracy in ancient Mesopotamia,," in Moran (1970) 157–70
Jacobsen, T. (1970b) "Early political development in Mesopotamia,," in Moran (1970).132–56.
Jacoby, F. (1949) *Atthis: The Local Chronicles of Ancient Athens* (Oxford)
Jones, N.F. (1991) "Enrollment clauses in Greek citizenship decrees," *ZPE* 87: 79–102.

Kahn, C.H. (1995) "The place of the *Statesman* in Plato's later work," in Rowe (1995) 49–60.
Kahn, C. H. (1973) *The Verb ‚be' in Ancient Greek* (Dordrecht/Boston).

Lehmann, G.A. (1995) "Überlegungen zu den oligarchischen Machtergreifungen im Athen des 4. Jahrhunderts v. Chr." in Eder (1995) 139–150.
Link, S. (1991) *Landverteilung und sozialer Frieden im archaischen Griechenland* (= *Historia* Einzelschrift 69) (Stuttgart).
Lord, C. & O'Connor, D.K. (edd.) (1991) *Essays on the Foundations of Aristotelian Political Science* (Berkeley, Los Angeles, and Oxford).
Lord, Carnes (tr.) (1984) *Aristotle: The Politics* (Chicago and London).

Maehler, H. *see under* Snell, B.
Moran, W.L. (ed.) (1970) *Toward the Image of Tammuz and Other Essays on Mesopotamian History and Culture* (Cambridge, MA),
Murray, O. (1980) *Early Greece* (London).

Newman, W.L. (1902) *The Politics of Aristotle* IV (Oxford).

Ober, J. and Hedrick, C.W. (edd.) (1996) *Demokratia: A Conversation on Democracies, Ancient and Modern* (Princeton).
Oliver, J.H. (1950) *The Athenian Expounders of the Sacred and Ancestral Law* (Baltimore)

Bibliography of Works Cited

Orsi, D.P. (1981) "Lessico politico: ὀλιγαρχία," *Quaderni di Storia* VII . 14: 135–150
Osborne, M.J. (1983) *Naturalization in Athens* IV:*Verhandelingen van de Koninklijke Academie voor Wetenschapen, Letteren en Schone Kunsten van Belgie* 45. No. 109.
Ostwald, M, (1986) *From Popular Sovereignty to the Sovereignty of Law* (Berkeley, Los Angeles, and London)
Ostwald, M. (1969) *Nomos and the Beginnings of the Athenian Democracy* (Oxford).
Ostwald, M. (1971) "The two states in Plato's *Republic*," in Anton, J.P. and Kustas, G.L. (1971) 316–27.
Ostwald, M. (1995) "Freedom and the Greeks," in Davis (ed.) (1995).
Ostwald, M. (1995a) "Public expense: Whose obligation?: Athens 600–454 B.C.E.," *Proceedings of the American Philosophical Society* 139: 368–79.
Ostwald, M. (1996) "Citizenship' Greek style and American style," in Ober, J. and Hedrick, C.W. (edd.) (1996) 49–61.

Page, D.L. (1955) *Sappho and Alcaeus* (Oxford).
Page, D.L. (1962) *Poetae Melici Graeci* (= *PMG*) (Oxford).
Pomeroy, Sarah B. (1994) *Xenophon* Oeconomicus: *A Social and Historical Commentary* (Oxford).

Raaflaub, K.A. (1998a) "The transformation of Athens," *Democracy, Empire, and the Arts in Fifth-Century Athens.* ed. by D. Boedeker & K. Raaflaub (Cambridge & London) 15–41.
Raaflaub, K.A. (1989) "Contemporary perceptions of democracy in fifth-century Athens," *Classica et Mediaevalia* 40: 37–41
Rackham, H. (tr.) (1944) *Aristotle: Politics* (London and Cambridge, MA).
Rhodes, P.J. (1981) *A Commentary on the Aristotelian* Athenaion Politeia (Oxford).
Rowe, C.J. (1995a) *Plato: Statesman* (Warminster).
Rowe, C.J. (ed.) (1995) *International Plato Studies* VI:4 *Reading the Statesman* .
Rusten, J.S. (ed.), (1989) *Thucydides: The Peloponnesian War. Book II* (Cambridge)

Salkever, S. G. (1991) "Aristotle's Social Science," in Lord, C. & O'Connor, D.K. (edd.) (1991) 11–48.
Sancisi-Weerdenburg, H.W.A.M. (1980) *Yauna en Persai. Grieken en Perzen in een Ander Perspectief* (diss. Leiden)
Schütrumpf, E. (1980) *Die Analyse der Polis durch Aristoteles* (Amsterdam)
Sickinger, J.P. (1999) *Public Records and Archives in Classical Athens* (Chapel Hill and London).
Simpson, P.L.P. (1998) *A Philoisophical Commentary on the* Politics *of Aristotle* (Chapel Hill, NC).
Snell, B. & Maehler, H (edd.) (1987) *Pindari Carmina* I: *Epinicia* (Leipzig).

Too, Yun Lee (1995) *The Rhetoric of Identity in Isocrates* (Cambridge).

Vernant, J.-P. (ed). (1968) *Problèmes de la guerre en Grèce ancienne* (Paris and The Hague)
Vidal-Naquet, P. (1968) "La tradition de l'hoplite athénien," in Vernant, J.-P. (ed) (1968) 161–81.
Vlachos, G. C. (1974) *Les sociétés politiques homériques* (Paris).

Walter, U. (1993) *An der Polis teilhaben: Bürgerstaat und Zugehörigkeit im Archaischen*

Walter, U. (1993) *An der Polis teilhaben: Bürgerstaat und Zugehörigkeit im Archaischen Griechenland* (*Historia* Einzelschrift 82) (Stuttgart).
Walzer, M. *Biblical Politics* (unpublished manuscript)
Weil, R. (1960) *Aristote et l'histoire: Essai sur la "Politique"* (Paris).
Weiss, E. (1923) *Griechisches Privatrecht* I (Leipzig).
Whibley, L. (1896) *Greek Oligarchies: Their Character and Organisation* (London).
White, S. A. (1992) *Sovereign Virtue: Aristotle on the Relation Between Happiness and Prosperity* (Stanford, CA).

Ziegler, K. (1951) "Plutarchos," *RE* 41. Halbb. 636–962.

GENERAL INDEX

Aeschines:
    democracy in: 29 and n.77
    oligarchy in: 29 and n. 77
affluence: 39, 42, 43, 44, 47;
    see also: εὔπορος
Agamemnon: 9
Alcaeus: 10
Alcibiades: 23
Alcinous: 9
Apollo: 13
Archilochus:
    tyranny in: 10, 17
archons: 27, 51, 53
Aristocracy:
    as government by the few: 31;
    in Plato: 33–34;
    in Aristotle: 37, 38–39, 42, 43, 57, 60, 63, 65
Aristotle: 41–75;
    on oligarchy: 12, 37, 38–39;
    relation to Plato: 37–38, 39–40, 48, 49
assemblies: 50;
    in Homer: 9;
    in democracies: 55, 74;
    low property valuation required in oligarchies: 70
Assyria: 14
Athenagoras: 25
Athens:
    in early sixth century: 11, 52;
    attitudes toward democracy in: 21, 50;
    assists democracies: 24;
    oligarchy in: 25–26, 27, 29;
    public register in: 51;
    property valuation in: 51–52;
    citizenship in: 53;
    proxenoi of: 61–62
    tyranny in: 62

Bacchiads: 23
Boeotian League:
    councils in: 27

Brasidas: 26

Carthage:
    appointment to office in: 58
Chios: 54
citizenship: 14, 38, 39, 40, 41, 44–49, 50–52, 52–53, 55–56, 57, 58, 64, 67, 68, 69, 70, 71–72, 75
classification by groups: 42 with n. 111, 56, 59
classification of constitutions:
    tripartite: 13, 15–20, 33–35 with n. 35;
    in Herodotus: 21;
    by Thrasymachus: 31;
    in Plato: 32, 33, 34–35;
    in Aristotle: 37–39, 56
Cleisthenes:
    and democracy: 11, 21;
    and political equality: 11
Colonus:
    meeting on in 411 B.C.E.: 25, 27
Colophon:
    oligarchy in: 72
common people:
    see under δῆμος
consent of the governed: 33
constitution:
    changes in: 62–63
"Constitutional Debate":
    in Herodotus: 14–15, 17–20, 23;
    historicity of: 14–15
Corcyra: 21–22, 24, 26
Corinth: 23
councils:
    in Boeotian League: 27;
    as pattern for Athens: 27
    attendance at meetings compulsory in oligarchies: 27;
    power of, eroded: 55;
    low property valuation required in oligarchies: 70

Crete:
   in Plato: 32, 34, 39
Cyclopes: 10

Daphnaeus: 62
Darius: 17–19
Deioces: 13
Delphi: 13
demagogues: 58
demes: 51
democracy:
   evolves from reforms of Cleisthenes: 11;
   opposition to, in Athens: 21 with nn. 37 and 38;
   opposed to tyranny: 21, 22–23;
   opposed to oligarchy: 21 with n. 38, 22–23;
   in Pericles' Funeral Oration: 22 with n. 40;
   threatened by profanations of 415 B.C.E.: 23, 25;
   affinity to Athens: 24;
   Aeschines on: 29 and n. 77;
   Demosthenes on: 29 and n. 77;
   Isocrates on: 28;
   in Plato: 32, 33–34;
   in Aristotle: 37, 38, 41, 42, 43, 44, 48, 63–64;
   types of: 55, 71, 73;
   property classes in: 50–52;
   ἄποροι and εὔποροι in: 57–58, 59, 64–65;
   is not majority rule: 43, 60;
   eligibility to office in: 67;
   stasis in: 68;
   citizenship in: 72, 74;
   defined by poverty: 75
Demosthenes:
   democracy in: 29 with n. 77;
   oligarchy in: 29 and n. 77
deviation: 38, 43;
   see also: παρέκβασις
Dexitheos: 61–62
Dionysius: 48, 62
dowry: 52, 61
dynasties: 11;
   see also: δυναστεία

Egypt: 14
elders:
   as oligarchical entity: 13–14
election:
   by lot: 37, 39, 70;
   by direct vote: 70
eligibility to office: 53, 67;
   determined by wealth in oligarchies: 25, 27, 59, 73;
   in oligarchies: 62, 63, 70–71, 75;
   property required for: 66, 69;
   in Athens 411 and 404 B.C.E.: 27;
   in Carthage: 58;
   in Aristotle: 39, 50, 58, 59;
   see also: "election"
embezzlement of public funds: 63, 65

equality:
   arithmetic and geometrical: 28–29;
   various kinds of: 42, 59, 67;
   of property: 47, 48–49, 58, 66, 74
Euripides: 21

few, the:
   definitions of: 23, 31;
   government by,
      in Plato: 32, 33–34;
      in Aristotle: 39, 41, 43, 66, 74–75
franchise, restriction of: 27
freedom:
   characteristic of democracy: 37, 39, 43, 44, 75;
   characteristic of polity: 67

Guardians: 32, 40
generals: 58;
   high property valuation of, in oligarchies: 70
Gyges: 72 n. 239

Herms, desecration of: 23
Herodotus: 11, 13, 14–15, 16, 23 with n. 43, 26;
   first to speak of "democracy" and "oligarchy": 11;
   account of monarchy in Media: 13;
   "Constitutional Debate" in: 14–15, 23;
   classification of constitutions in: 21;
   conflates oligarchy and aristocracy: 23

Hesiod: 10
Hippodamus of Miletus: 55
Histiaea: 49 n. 139, 61
Hittites: 14
honours: 63
hoplites: 42

ideology:
    see: "propaganda and ideology"
indigence: 39, 42, 44, 54;
    see also: ἄπορος
inheritance laws: 48-49 with n.139, 61, 64
interest of the governed: 22, 31, 38, 39, 63, 65
interest of the rulers: 31, 38, 63-64, 65, 69, 73
Isocrates: 28-29
Israel:
    monarchy in ancient: 13-14
Issedonians: 53 n. 164
Ithaca: 9

jury service: 39, 55, 67;
    low property valuation required in oligarchies: 70
justice:
    as criterion for constitutions: 31
    distributive, in Aristotle: 41

Kennedy, John F.: 65
kingship:
    in Homer: 9;
    in Hesiod: 10
    in early lyric: 10-11;
    in Assyria: 14;
    among Hittites: 14;
    in Israel: 14;
    in Media: 13;
    in Mesopotamia: 14;
    in Persia: 14, 18-20;
    among Phoenicians: 14;
    in Isocrates: 28-29;
    in Plato: 34;
    in Aristotle: 37, 38, 39, 42;
    see also: "monarchy"
Knossos: 9
Kronos: 9

Laconian oligarchy: 39
law-abiding: 33, 34, 37, 38, 39
lawagetai: 9
laws (written): 33. 38, 63, 70-71, 73
leisure: 53, 55, 58, 59, 60, 63, 71
Lincoln, Abraham: 65 n. 194
liturgies: 52, 57, 64
Lydia: 72

majority rule: 25, 39, 40, 43, 59, 60, 66
Media: 13
Megabyzus: 17-19, 21, 26
Megara:
    in early sixth century: 11;
    stasis in: 26;
    πρόβουλοι in: 26. 27;
    Theagenes, tyrant of: 62
Menelaus: 9
merit:
    as criterion in public appointments: 23, 28, 40, 41, 58, 60
Mesopotamia: 14
Messenian Wars: 62
metics: 53
middle class: 58, 67;
    see also: μέσος
Miletus: 54, 55
military units: 63
"mixed constitution": 38, 58
monarchy:
    in Near East: 13-14;
    Isocrates on: 28-29;
    in Plato: 33-34;
    in Aristotle: 37, 73;
    see also: "kingship"
monopoly: 54-55
Mycenae: 9
Mysteries, profanation of: 23
Mytilene: 10-11;
    revolt of: 61-62 with nn. 190 and 191

Nicias: 24-25
Nicocles: 28

Odysseus: 9
oikistes: 13
"Old Oligarch": 23-24, 25

oligarchy: 66, 74–75;
   Aeschines on: 29 and n. 77;
   in Aristotle: 37, 38, 39–40, 42, 43–44, 50, 63;
   Demosthenes on: 29 and n. 77;
   in fourth-century orators: 28 with n. 68;
   in Herodotus: 18–20;
   Isocrates on: 28;
   in "Old Oligarch": 23–24;
   in Pindar: 16;
   in Plato: 32, 33–35;
   in Athens: 23, 25, 26, 27;
   and Sparta: 24; 70;
   two kinds of in Thebes: 25–26;
   and property:12, 44–49, 50, 51;
   defined by wealth: 69, 75;
   opposed to democracy: 21;
   as government for the few: 22;
   ἄποροι and εὔποροι in: 57–58, 59, 64, 65;
   four kinds of: 70–71, 73;
   not minority rule: 43, 60, 66;
   citizenship in: 71–75;
   eligibility to office in: 67, 69;
   revolutionary change in: 55, 62, 68
"One Hundred": 70
Oracle at Delphi: 13
Otanes: 17–19

payment for office: 44, 45, 51, 55, 68;
   not oligarchical: 25;
   suspended at Athens in 411 B.C.E.: 27;
   for jury duty: 39, 55
Peisander: 26
Peisistratus: 11, 62
Peloponnesian War: 24, 26
pentakosiomedimnoi:: 51
pentarchia : 70
Pericles:
   democratic policies of: 23 n. 43;
   democracy in Funeral Oration of: 22, 65 n. 194
Persia: 13, 14, 17;
   "Constitutional Debate" in: 14–15, 17–20;
   as tyrannical society: 21

Persian Wars: 21, 25, 61
Phaeacia: 9
Phaleas of Chalcedon: 47 with n. 132, 48
philosopher, rule of: 32–35
Phoenicians: 14
phratry: 63
Pindar:
   tripartite classification of constitutions in: 15–17;
   rule of the few in: 21, 23 with n. 43
Pittacus: 10–11
Plataea: 25
Plato: 22
   influence on Aristotle: 37–38, 39–40, 48, 49, 68
political equality (in Athens): 11;
   see also: ἰσονομία
polity:
   in Aristotle: 38–40, 42, 55, 59, 60, 63, 67
poverty: 54, 65, 75;
   see also: πένης, πενία
priesthoods: 53, 57
probouloi: 27
propaganda and ideology: 22, 24–25, 26, 28, 30, 41
property:
   in Plato: 32, 33, 46;
   in Aristotle: 37, 39–40, 42, 44–49, 57, 61–65, 68;
   class: *see under*: τέλος;
   equality of: 58, 65;
   imbalance in: 58;
   slaves as: 53;
   valuation of: 45, 47, 50–52, 59, 69–70;
   and citizenship: 71–75;
   and public service: 70;
   and oligarchy: 70–75;
   see also: "wealth"
prosperity:
   as characteristic of tyrant: 16, 17
proxenos: 61–62
prytaneis: 27
Pylos: 9

revolution: 24, 26, 41, 48, 55, 74;
   of Mytilene: 61

"rights": 52–53
Romans: 14
royal expert: 32–33, 34–35, 38, 39

Samuel: 13
Samos: 27
Saul: 13
Sicilian Expedition: 23, 27
Sikyon:
    oligarchy in: 26 n. 55
slaves: 46, 48, 49, 52
"Smerdis": 14, 21
Socrates:
    response to Thrasymachus: 22, 31
Solon: 11, 17, 50, 51–52, 59
Sparta:
    Menelaus, king of: 9;
    Messenian War: 62;
    allied with oligarchies: 24;
    war-aims of, in Peloponnesian War: 24–25;
    disparity of property in: 47, 48;
    oligarchical elements in constitution of: 70;
    called "timocracy" by Plato: 32
stasis: 60–62, 68;
    in Corcyra: 21–22, 24, 26, 47
Syracuse: 25, 48, 62

Ten, The: 27
Thales: 54
Theagenes: 62
Thebes:
    two kinds of oligarchy in: 25–26
Theognis: 11
thetes: 52, 59, 69
Thirty, The: 27, 32
Thrasymachus: 22, 31, 38
Thucydides: 24–26, 29;
    on *stasis* in Corcyra: 21–22, 24;
    Pericles in: 22;
    on profanation of the Mysteries: 23;
    on Nicias: 24–25;
    Thebes in: 25–26
timocracy:
    in Plato: 32;
    in Aristotle: 39–40

Timophanes: 61–62
treasurers: 57, 70
tribe: 63
trierarchs: 27
tyranny:
    developed from family dynasties: 11;
    in Athens: 11, 23;
    in Alcaeus: 10–11;
    in Archilochus: 10, 17;
    in Aristotle: 37, 38, 42, 58, 62, 66;
    in Herodotus: 17;
    in Plato: 32, 33, 34
tyrants:
    prosperity as characteristic of: 16, 17;
    Dionysius of Syracuse: 48, 62;
    Peisistratus of Athens: 11, 62;
    Pittacus of Mytilene: 10–11;
    Theagenes of Megara: 62;
    in Aristotle: 48, 58;
    in Isocrates: 29;
    in Plato: 32, 34

United States:
    constitution of: 44

wanaktes: 9
wealth:
    as hallmark of the few: 24, 75;
    defines oligarchy: 69, 71, 72, 73, 75;
    prerequisite for office in oligarchies: 25, 27, 67;
    and *stasis*: 68;
    and polity: 67;
    and tyranny: 62;
    in Aristotle: 37, 39, 42, 43–44, 54–55, 57, 59, 60, 63, 65, 66, 69;
    in Plato: 32, 33, 34
well-to-do:
    see under: „affluence", εὔπορος
Whibley, Leonard: 11–12
women:
    excluded from full citizenship: 53

zeugitai: 59
Zeus: 10

INDEX LOCORUM

Aeschines
  I (T*im.*) 4–5: 29 n.77
  III (*Ctes.*) 6: 29 n.76;
        168: 29 n.77;
        169: 29 n.77;
        170: 29 n.77;
        220: 29 n.77;
        233: 29 n.75

Alcaeus
  frr. (L.-P.) 6. 27: 10 n.7;
        75: 10 n.7;
        348: 10 n.7

Antiphon
  V (*Herodes*) 77: 52 n.161;
  fr. (Blass-Thalheim) 61: 52 n.160

Archilochus
  frr. (West) 19: 10 n.6, 16 n.21;
        19. 3: 17 n.25;
        23. 20: 10 n.6,16 n.21

Aristophanes
  Acharnenses 755: 26 n.54

Aristotle
  Athenaion Politeia 7. 3: 50 n.144,
        51 n.155;
        7. 3–4: 51 n.154,
        52 n.159;
        8. 1: 51 n.155;
        14.1: 13 n.13;
        29.2: 27 n.65;
        29.5: 27 nn.56,
          57, 60, and 64;
        30.2: 27 n.60;
        30.3: 27;
        31.1: 27 n.63;
        36.1: 27 n.58
  Politica I. 1, 1252a18–23: 56 with
        n.172;

Politica I. (ctd.)
  4, 1253b23–24: 46 n.128;
    1253b31–32: 46 n.128;
    1253b32: 46 n.124;
    1254a2–5: 45 n.122;
    1254a10–17: 46 n.124;
  7, 1266a37–40: 46 n.132;
  8, 1256a16–17: 46 n.128;
    1256b4–8: 46 n.129;
    1256b31–32: 46 n.129;
  9, 1257a6–16: 45 n.122;
    1257b14–15: 54
    1257b35–1258a1: 49;
    1258a2–6: 46 n.128;
  10, 1258b2–4: 46 n.130;
  11, 1258b13–16: 46 n.126;
    1259a6–19: 55, 57 n.
      178;
    1259a22: 55 n.171;
  13, 1259b19–21: 46 n.127;
II. 1, 1261a6–8: 46 n.131;
  3, 1261b20–27: 48;
  5, 1263b1–3: 46 n.131;
    1263b11–14: 46 n.123;
    1263b15–27: 48;
    1263b39–1264a16: 46
      n.131;
  6, 1265a28–39: 46 n.132
    1265a31–b11: 48
      n.137;
    1265b21–23: 49;
    1266a8–13: 51 n.157;
    1266a9–10: 70 n.224;
    1266a12–14: 50
      n.147;
    1266a13–14: 70
      n.221;
    1266a16–17: 51n.154;
  7, 1266a37–40: 47;
    1266b8–13: 48 n.137,
      49 n.140;
    1266b14–33: 49;

Politica II. (ctd.)
    1266b23–24: 51 nn.156 and 157;
    1266b25: 50 n.142;
    1266b25–33: 48;
    1266b40–67a10: 48;
    1267a28–37: 49;
    1267a37–b9: 72;
    1267b9–10: 46 n.132;
    1267b9–13: 48;
    1267b10–12: 46 n.126;
  8, 1268a41–b1: 55;
  9, 1270a15–18: 47, 48;
    1270b9–10: 45 n.118, 54 n.168;
    1271a29–37: 55 n.170;
 11, 1273a13–17: 70 n.226;
    1273a23–25: 58;
    1273a24–25: 45 n.118, 54 n.168;
    1273a25–26: 69 n.214;
    1273a26: 69 n.206, 72 n.241;
    1273a35–36: 53;
    1273a35–39: 58;
    1273b5–7: 59 n.180;
    1273b6–7: 53;
 12, 1274b9–11: 48 n.138;
    1274b15–21: 59;
III. 1, 1275a5–19: 53;
    1275a22–23: 53 n.165;
  3, 1276b6–9: 56 n.172;
  4, 1277a8: 46 n.125;
    1277a37–b1: 53;
  5, 1278a8–11: 53 n.166;
    1278a21–23: 50 n.147;
    1278a21–25: 69 n.213;
    1278a21–26: 51 n.157;
    1278a23: 51 n.156, 70 n.220;
    1278a24: 69 n.215;
    1278a29–34: 56;
  6, 1278b11: 42 n.109;

Politica III. (ctd.)
  7, 1279a22–b10: 38 n.97;
    1279a25–31: 42 n.109, 65 n.193;
    1279a22–b10: 38 n.97;
    1279b5: 43;
    1279b7–10: 45 n.119, 65 n.194;
    1279b8: 69 n.210, 73 n.245;
  8, 1279b11–1280a6: 66 n.195;
    1279b17–18: 69 n.209, 73 n.244;
    1279b17–19: 44 n.114, 66, 72 n.236;
    1279b20–26: 43 n.113;
    1279b28–31: 59, 67 n.200;
    1279b34–1280a4: 75 n.253;
    1279b39–1280b6: 45 n.120, 66 n.197;
    1280a1–2: 69 n.206, 72 n.241;
  9, 1280a25–27: 46 n.128;
  9–13: 41;
 11, 1282a29: 52 n.158;
    1282a29–31: 51 n.157, 70 n.219;
    1282a31–32: 51 n.156, 70 n.221;
 12, 1283a18–19: 45 n.118, 54 n.168;

Politica III. (ctd.)
    17, 1288a13–15: 60
        n.184;
  IV. 2, 1289a38–b5: 42;
      1289a38–b9: 43
        n.112;
      3–4: 56 n.173;
      3–10: 41;
      3, 1289b27–28: 56
        n.172;
      1289b27–1290a5:
        42 n.110,
        56 n.175;
      1290a7–11:
        42 n.111;
      1290a7–13:
        59 n.181;
      1290a13–18: 42;
      1290a27–29:
        70 n.222;
      4, 1290a24–29:
        43 n.112;
      1290a30–40:
        60 n.186;
      1290a30–b3:
        43 n.113, 59
        n.183, 60,
        66 n.195,
        69 n.205,
        72 n.240;
      1290a33–b3:
        66 n.197;
      1290a34–35: 60;
      1290b3: 60;
      1290b15–17: 72;
      1290b20:
        69 n.211;
      1290b23–24:
        56 n.172;
      1290b38–39:
        56 n.172;
      1291a33–34:
        56, 57, 75;
      1291b2–8:
        54 n.169, 57
        n.178;
      1291b7–8: 55;
      1291b7–13:

Politica IV. (ctd.)
        69 n.208, 72
        n.243;
      1291b25–26:
        71 n.232;
      1291b30–34:
        67 n.201;
      1291b39–40:
        50 n.146, 51
        n.156, 70
        n.219;
      5, 1292a29–41:
        71 n.228;
      5, 1292a39–40:
        50 n.143,
        51 n.156,
        69 n.218;
      1292a39–b4:
        50 n.147;
      1292a41:
        50 n.142;
      1292b1:
        51 n.156, 70
        n.220;
      1292b1–3:
        51 n.157;
      1292b1–4:
        71 n.229;
      1292b5–7:
        71 n.231;
      6, 1292b25–29:
        71 n.233;
      1292b29–30:
        69 n.217;
      1292b29–31:
        72 n.234;
      1292b30:
        51 n.148;
      1292b30–32:
        50 n.142;
      1292b31–32:
        50 n.143;
      1292b31–33:
        69 n.212;
      1292b41–
        1293a11: 55;
      1293a12–34:
        73 n.248;

Politica IV. (ctd.)
 1293a13–20: 71 n.228;
 1293a21–26: 71 n.229;
 1293a26–30: 71 n.230;
 1293a30–32: 71 n.231;
8–9: 38–39;
8, 1293b23ff: 43 n.112;
 1293b33–34: 39;
 1293b36–40: 61 n.188;
 1293b41–42: 69 n.211, 73 n.247;
 1294a11: 43 n.113, 69 nn.205 and 207, 72 nn.240 and 242;
 1294a11–14: 43 n.113;
 1294a15–23: 39;
 1294a16–19: 67;
 1294a18–19: 69 n.211, 73 n.247;
 1294a30–b13: 39;
9, 1294a37–41: 67, 70 n.225;
 1294a37–42: 59 n.182;
 1294b3–4: 50 n.146, 51 n.157, 52 n.158;
 1294b4: 50 n.147;
 1294b4–5: 71 n.230;
 1294 b8–9: 70 n.222;
 1294b9–10: 51 n.156;
 1294b10:

Politica IV. (ctd.)
 39 n.102, 69 n.215;
 1294b19: 39;
 1294b34–40: 39 n.100;
10: 50 n.147;
11, 1295b1–3: 56 n.174, 67;
 1295b39–40: 72;
 1296a7–18: 58;
 1296a25: 72;
 1296a27–32: 60, 68;
12, 1296b13–34: 42 n.111;
 1296b24–34: 67;
 1296b31–33: 69 n.211, 73 n.247;
 1297a7–13: 60 n.187;
 1297a11–12: 63;
13, 1297a14–b1: 67 n.202;
 1297a17–19: 70 n.223;
 1297a17–35: 27 n.64;
 1297a19–22: 70 n.225;
 1297b6–8: 71;
 1297b6–12: 59 n.182;
14–16: 41;
14, 1298a35–40: 71 n.228;
 1298a38–40: 50 n.142;
 1298a40–b2: 71 n.229;
 1298b2–5: 71 n.230;
 1298b29: 27 n.66;
15, 1299a24: 59 n.183;
 1299b25–26:

Politica V. (ctd.)
69 n.214;
1299b31–36:
27 n.66;
1299b38–
1300a4: 55;
V. 1, 1301a31–33: 74;
1301b39–
1302a2: 57
n.179;
3, 1302b25–29: 68;
1303a1–2:
68 n.204;
1303a10–13:
68 n.204;
1303a11–13:
72 n.235;
4: 45 n.119;
4, 1303b34–37:
45 n.119,
49 n.139,
61 n.189;
1304a4–10:
61 n.190;
5–12: 41;
5, 1304b20–24: 48;
1305a3–7: 48;
1305a21–28: 62;
1305a29–30:
51 n.156,
52 n.158;
1305a30–31:
51 n.157;
6, 1305b1–10: 62;
1305b32–33:
51 n.157;
1306a2–4: 62;
1306b3–16:
47 n.133;
1306b7–9:
70 n.219;
1306b8–9:
39 n.102, 69
n.216;
1306b12–13:
50 n.142;
7, 1306b36–1307a2:
62;

Politica V. (ctd.)
1307a19–27: 63;
1307a27–28:
50 n.143;
1307a35–36:
47 n.135, 48;
8, 1307b33–34: 48;
1308a35–38: 55;
1308a35–b4:
51 n.149;
1308b25–31: 58;
1308b31–
1309a32: 64
n.192;
1309a25–26: 49;
9, 1309b38–1310a6:
58;
1309b39–
1310a2: 49;
10, 1310b40–
1311a2: 48;
11, 1315a31–40: 58;
1313b25–28: 48;
12, 1316b1–3:
45 n.116,
74 n.249;
1316b6–14:
68 n.203;
1316b18–25: 48;
VI. 2, 1317b8–10: 67;
1317b22:
51 n.156;
1317b22–23: 50
n.146, 52
n.158,
70 n.219;
1317b30–35: 55;
1317b38–41:
69 n.211;
1318a6–8:
67 n.201;
3, 1318a20:
69 n.209;
1318a20–21:
45 n.116,
74 n.250;
1318a23–24:
66 n.198;

2. Index Locorum

Politica VI. (ctd.)
   1318a24–26:
     66 n.199;
   1318a30–38:
     51 n.157;
   4, 1318b30–31:
     51 n.156;
   1319a17–19:
     47 n.133;
   5, 1320a24–b4:
     67 n.202;
   1320a36–39:
     46 n.132;
   6–8: 41;
   6, 1320b18–33:
     70 n.227;
   1320b21–24:
     70 n.221;
   1320b25–26:
     50 n.142;
   7, 1321a12–13:
     56 n.175;
   1321a28:
     50 n.142;
   8, 1322b16:
     27 n.66;
   1323a9: 27 n.66;
VII. 5, 1326b30–36:
     45 n.118,
     53 n.167;
   1326b33–36:
     47 n.136;
   1326b34:
     46 n.132;
   6, 1327a18–20: 55;
   8, 56 n.173;
   1328a21–27:
     56 n.172;
   1328a33–35:
     46 n.127;
   1328b5–23:
     57 n.177;
   1328b10–11: 55;
   9, 1329a18:
     46 n.132;
   1329a18–21:
     44 n.114,
     45 n.118,
     53 n.167;

Politica VII. (ctd.)
   1329a25:
     46 n.132;
   10, 1329b41–1330a2:
     46 n.131;
   1330a1–8: 55;
   1330a30–31: 49;
   11, 1295b3–5:
     46 n.132;
   13, 1332 a15–16: 60;
   VIII. 6, 1341a28–29: 60;

Ethica Nicomachea
   VIII. 10, 1160a31–b22: 39
     with n.101;
   1160b12–16: 40;
   1160b17–19: 40
     n.103

Rhetorica
   I. 8, 1365b21–1366a16:
     37 n.95;
   1365b33:
     50 nn.143
     and 147,
     51 n.156

Attic Skolia
   (Page, *PMC*) 893.4: 11 n.10;
     896.4: 11 n.10

Demosthenes
   XV (*Rhod.*) 17: 29 n.77;
     18: 29 n.77;
     19: 29 n.77;
     21: 29 n.77;
   XIX (*Falsa Leg.*) 184: 29 n.76;
   XX (*Leptines*) 15: 29 n.76;
   XXII (*Androtion*) 51: 29 n.77;
   XXIV (*Timocrates*) 75: 29 n.77
     76: 29 n.77;
     144: 51
     n.154;
     149: 29 n.76;
   XXVII (*Aphobus* 1) 7: 50 n.142;
   XXIX (*Aphobus* 3) 60: 50 n.142;
   XLIII (*Macartatus*) 54: 51 n.154,
     52 n.162

Euripides
   Supplices 403–55: 21;
     421–5: 53 n.166

Harpocration
svv. θῆτες: 52 nn.159 and 160
Θητικόν: 52 nn.159 and 160
ἱππάς: 51 n.154, 52 n.159

Hellenica Oxyrynchia
(Chambers) 19.2: 27 n.62

Herodotus
I. 14.4: 72 n.239;
59.5–6: 13 n.13;
96.2: 13 n.13;
97.2–3: 13 n.13;
III. 38.1: 11 n.11;
80–82: 14;
80.2–5: 18;
80.4: 17, 18 n.26;
80.6: 17, 19 n.31;
81.1: 18, 19 n.32, 26;
81.2: 17;
81.3: 18 n.30, 23, 26;
82.1: 18;
82.2: 18 n.27;
82.3: 18;
82.4: 18, 19 n.33;
82.5: 18 n.28;
83.2: 18;
84.1–3: 18;
IV. 26.2: 53 n.164;
V. 78: 11 n.10;
92β1: 23;
VI. 43.3: 14, 17

Hesiod
Opera et Dies 248–73: 10 n.5

Hesychius
s.vv. ἐκ τιμημάτων: 50 n.144;
ζευγίσιον: 50 n.144;
ἱππάδα: 50 n.144;
ὁμοτελεῖς: 51 n.154;
Θητικόν: 50 n.144

Homer
Iliad II. 199–206: 9 n.3;
Odyssey IX.106–114: 10

Homeric *Hymn to Demeter* 473–82: 10 n.5

Isaeus
VII (*Apollodorus*) 39: 51 nn.149 and 154

Isocrates
III (*Nicocles*) 14: 28 n.70;
15: 28 nn.71 and 72;
VIII (*De Pace*) 133: 28 n.69;
XII (*Panath..*) 132: 29 n.73

Lysias
XIX (*Aristophanes*) 48: 51 n.149;
XVII (*Erat.*) 7–9: 51 n.150;
XXV (*Reipubl. Ev.*) 8: 28 n.69

Pindar
Olympians
II. 87: 16;
VIII. 36: 16;
Pythians
II.: 15 n.19;
86–88: 15, 15 nn.19 and 20;
III. 40: 16;
85: 16;
IV. 244: 16;
295: 16 n.22;
IX. 78: 16 n.22;
XI. 53: 16

Plato
Epistulae VII. 324b–325c: 32 n.83;
326a–b: 31 n.79;
Leges III. 698b: 51 n.154;
IV.710e3–7: 34 n.92;
712b8–c5: 34 n.91;
712c3–5: 34 n.93;
712e9–713a2: 34 n.91;
V. 744a–d: 50 n.142, 51 n.154;
VIII. 832b10–c3: 34 n.91;
X. 915b: 50 n.142;
Politicus 291d–301a: 33;
292a5–a8: 33;
292c5–293a1: 33;
293d4–e5: 34;

Politicus (ctd.)
    297c–303b: 38 n.97;
    301a6–a8: 34 n.90;
    301c1–c3: 33;
    301d8–e4: 33 n.87;
    302e1–2: 33 n.88;
    302e4–8: 33 n.87;
    303a7–8: 33 n.89;
Respublica I. 338d7–8: 31 n.78;
    341a–342e: 22 n.41;
    IV. 444e-445e: 31 n.80;
    VIII. 544c–545a: 39;
    544c1–IX. 588a11: 32;
    544d1–4: 32 n.84;
    544e7: 32;
    545b7–550d3: 32 n.84;
    545c8–548d5: 32 n.81;
    550c–551c: 40 n.104;
    550c8–555b2: 32 n.82;
    550c–d: 50 n.143;
    VIII. 551b: 50 nn.142 and 143;
    553a: 50 n.143

Plutarch
    Aristides 13.1: 21 n.37;
    Moralia 826a–827c: 20 n.35

Polybius
    VI. 3–4: 14

Pollux
    VIII. 130–131: 52 n.159

Polyaenus
    VII.1: 13 n.13

Samuel II
    8: 4–5: 13;
    7: 13

Solon
    frr.(West) 9.3–4: 11 n.9;
    32.2: 11 n.9;
    33.6: 11 n.9, 17 n.25;
    34.7: 11 n.9

Suda
    s.vv. ἐκ τιμημάτων: 50 n.144;
    ἱππάς: 52 n.159

Theognis
    823: 11 n.9;
    1181: 11 n.9;
    1204: 11 n.9

Thucydides
    I. 19.1: 25 n.47;
    II. 37.1: 22 n.40, 65 n.194;
    III. 2–6: 61 n.190;
    8–18: 61 n.190;
    27: 62 n.191;
    47.2: 24 n.46;
    62.3: 25 n.49;
    82.1: 25 n.47;
    82.8: 22 and n. 42, 25 n.49;
    IV. 74.3–4: 25 n.47;
    74.4: 26 n.55;
    V. 31.6: 25 n.47;
    38. 2–3: 27 n. 63;
    81.2: 25 n.47, 26 n.55;
    VI. 11.7: 25 n.47;
    39: 25;
    43: 52 n.160;
    60.1: 21 n.38, 23, 25;
    VIII. 47.2: 25, 27 n.61;
    53.1: 26 n.52;
    53.3: 26 n.53;
    54.1: 26 n.52;
    64.1–2: 26 n.55;
    64.3: 22 n.42;
    65.3: 27 nn.56, 57, and 60;
    67.3: 25 n.48, 27 nn.60 and 63;
    97.1: 27 n.57

Xenophon
    Hellenica II. 3.18: 27 n.58;
    Memorabilia IV. 6. 12: 51 n.156;
    Oeconomicus II. 6: 52 n.161;

Xenophon (ctd.)
    [*Athenaion Politeia*] I. 2: 24;
                      5–6: 24;
                      9–12: 24;
              II. 17: 23 n.45;
                  20: 23 n.45

GREEK INDEX

ἀναρχία: 68
ἄνοπλον, τὸ: 56
ἄπορος, ἀπορία, ἀπορεῖν: 44, 49 and
  n.139, 54–68, 74;
  τῶν καρπῶν: 55;
  τροφῆς: 55;
  in material goods: 54–56;
  in social and economic matters:
    56–57;
  in professional life: 57;
  and citizenship: 58, 69, 72;
  and πένης: 59, 60, 63, 65;
  and eligibility to office: 67
ἀρετή, ἄριστος: 21 n. 36
ἀριστοκρατία: 22, 23, 29 and n. 73
  in Plato: 31, 32, 33
ἀταξία: 68

βάναυσος τεχνίτης: 53, 69
βασιλεία, βασιληίη, βασιλεύς: 17 with
  n. 24 18, 29, 37 n. 94
βασιλικός: 33

γενναῖος: 24
γνώριμος: 61, 69, 73

δέξιος: 24
δεύτερος πλοῦς: 33
δημοκρατεῖσθαι, δημοκρατία: 17, 24
δῆμος: 17, 60, 62, 68, 72
δίκαιον: 74
δυναστεία: 25, 71, 73
δυνατός: 24

ἐλευθερίη: 18 n. 28
ἐξηγηταὶ πυθόχρηστοι: 14
ἐπιστήμη: 33
ἐργασία: 48, 57
εὔπορος, εὐπορία, εὐπορεῖν: 44, 45, 49
  and n. 139, 52–68
  τῶν ἀναγκαίων: 55;
  μισθοῦ: 55;

νομίσματος: 55;
ὄχλου: 56;
προσόδων: 55;
χρημάτων: 54, 55;
in material goods: 54–56;
in social and economic matters: 56–
  57:
in professional life: 57;
and citizenship: 58, 72, 73–75;
and πλούσιος: 59, 60, 63, 65, 69;
stasis among: 62, 68;
and eligibility to office: 67;
see also: "affluence"

θῆτες:
  see under : "*thetes*"

ἰσονομία:
  ἰσονομία πολιτική: 22;
  see also under : "political equality"
ἰσόνομος: 25

κακία: 40
καλὸς κἀγαθός: 39, 69, 73
κρεῖττον: 68
κριταὶ τῶν ἀναγκαίων καὶ συμφερόντων: 57
κτάομαι: 46
κτῆμα: 45–46, 48, 66
κτῆσις: 45–49, 66
  τῆς γῆς: 48
  ἀνωμαλία τῆς: 48

λαβρός: 16
λήξεις: 37
ληξιαρχικὸν γραμματεῖον: 51

μέσοι: 56;
  see also: "middle class"
μισθός: 67;
  see also: "payment for office"

μο(ύ)ναρχος, μο(υ)ναρχί(η)α: 10 n. 7,
17 with n. 24, 18, 29 and n. 73, 37 n.
94

οἰκία: 42, 56
ὀλιγαρχίη, ὀλιγαρχία: 17, 18, 23, 24,
26, 34;
ὀλιγαρχία ἰσόνομος: 25
ὅμιλος, ὁμιλίη: 17, 23
ὁπλιτικόν, τὸ: 56
ὀρθός: 38
οὐσία: 45, 47 n. 134, 47–49, 50, 66, 70,
74–75;
ἴδιοι τῶν κεκτημένων τὰς: 49;
ἰσότης τῆς: 48, 72;
οἱ κεκτημένοι τὰς: 48, 66;
μέση καὶ ἱκανή: 72;
τοῦ νομίσματος: 49;
ὁμαλότης τῆς: 49;
ταῖς οὐσίαις λειτουργεῖν: 56;
τὴν πᾶσαν: 49;
πλῆθος οὐσίας: 49, 66
πολλὴν λίαν: 47, 48

παρέκβασις: 38, 65
πένης, πενία, πένεσθαι: 44, 54–56, 60,
65, 66, 67
see also : "poverty"
πλείους: 68
πλῆθος ἄρχον: 17
πλούσιος, πλοῦτος, πλουτεῖν: 23, 44,
54–56, 60, 62, 65, 66, 67, 69, 72;

see also: "wealth"
πόλις βελτίστη: 54
πολιτεία:
ἀρίστη: 37 n. 96;
μετέχειν τῆς πολιτείας: 50, 52
in Aristotle: 38
πολίτευμα: 42 n. 109
πολιτικόν: 33
γένος πολιτικόν: 59
πρακτικόν: 45
πρόβουλοι: 26, 27

στάσεις καὶ μάχαι: 60–61;
see also: "*stasis*"

τεκνοποιία: 48
τέλος: 50–52, 70
τιμή: 39, 60
τίμημα: 39, 47, 50–52 with n. 142, 69,
70–71;
see also: "property, valuation of"
τίμησις: 51
τιμοκρατία: 39
τυραννίς, τύραννος: 15–16, 17 with n.
24, 18, 29 and n. 73, 37 n. 94;
see also: "tyranny", "tyrants"

ὕβρις: 17, 18, 19 with n. 34, 20, 22

φιλία: 39

χρηστός: 23